P9-CEG-090

The *Truth* about Texas

Anne Dingus

Gulf Publishing Company
Houston, Texas

This is a revised edition. The first edition was published under the title *The Dictionary of Texas Misinformation*. Copyright 1987 by Anne Dingus.

Gulf Publishing Company
Book Division
P.O. Box 2608 ☐ Houston Texas 77252-2608

10   9   8   7   6   5   4   3   2   1

Library of Congress Cataloging-in-Publication Data

Dingus, Anne, 1953–
    [Dictionary of Texas misinformation]
    The truth about Texas : who needs to brag? We've got the facts / Anne Dingus. — Rev. ed.
        p. cm.
    Original title: The Dictionary of Texas misinformation.
    Includes bibliographical references.
    ISBN 0-87719-282-0
    1. Texas—History—Dictionaries.   I. Title.
F386.D56   1995
976.4'003—dc20   95-12594
                                        CIP

ACKNOWLEDGMENTS

Many agencies and organizations helped to clarify and verify material for this book, particularly the Texas Department of Agriculture, Texas Parks and Wildlife, and the Texas Highway Department. The staffs of the Eugene C. Barker Texas History Center and the Legislative Library were especially helpful.

The author also thanks William D. King, John Reese Thomas, and William F. Dingus, who shared their areas of expertise; Lorraine Atherton, who edited and improved the manuscript; and Patrick D. Redman, who provided advice and encouragement along the way.

INTRODUCTION

Misinformation is an old Texas tradition. Before Texas was even a republic, prospective immigrants heard mixed reports of its attractions and dangers. The Alamo martyrs, cowboys, and Indians quickly colored America's perception of Texas as a crude and lawless land—a reputation that money, cattle, and oil did nothing to dispel. To the rest of the world, Texas is something less than civilized.

We Texans exaggerate in the opposite direction—as if we needed to. What is a brag, after all, except misinformation we're picky about? To us, everything about Texas spells romance, valor, and adventure. We embrace our mythology as fervently as our history, and the two are so intertwined that separating truth from falsehood sometimes seems impossible.

But facts are facts. Not everyone in the Alamo died. Not everyone in Texas is a cowboy. More than three-quarters of all Texans live in cities, and Texas had more than six flags. *The Truth About Texas* examines folklore, trivia, and entire legends that are misleading, misunderstood, or just plain wrong. The author sympathizes with fellow Texans who prefer the time-honored, if untrue, versions and, though she welcomes corrections and commentary, asks that the reader interpret any misinformation herein not as further proof of Texan fallibility but as evidence of her own native loyalty.

Aggie

Aggies—that is, students at Texas A&M University in College Station—have long gotten a raw deal in terms of the public's opinion of their intellect. In fact, A&M is highly regarded by the academic community nationwide. The university makes the top ten nationally in four major areas: overall enrollment (#3); entering National Merit Scholars (#4); total value of its research programs (#7); and endowment (#6). In 1994 the average combined Scholastic Aptitude Test (SAT) score for entering freshmen was 1,078—194 points higher than the statewide average.

Despite their persistent hayseed image, as many Aggies are urban as rural. The majority of native students hail from the counties of Harris, Dallas, and Bexar—in other words, Houston, Dallas, and San Antonio. The cosmopolitan school also draws students from the 49 other states and from 115 foreign countries. And though Aggies in jokes are inevitably male, today 43 percent of A&M's enrollment is female.

Hotshots on the Aggie faculty include two Nobel winners—Dr. Norman Borlaug (1970 peace prize) and Sir Derek Barton (1969 chemistry prize)—as well as two Pulitzer recipients—Charles Gordone (drama, 1970) and Douglas Starr (part of a general reporting team, 1954).

See **Texas A&M University.**

Agriculture

Though agriculture was Texas' leading industry for more than 100 years, it is no longer. Since the forties the oil and gas industry has generated more income. Texas entered World War II as an agriculturally based state and emerged as a petroleum-centered one.

Texas doesn't harvest more acres of crops than any other state. Though more than 20 million acres are harvested here, Iowa, Illinois, Kansas, North Dakota, and Minnesota harvest more. But Texas boasts a greater variety of crops and grains. And though Texas has far more farms than any other state—180,644—the average one contains only about 725 acres, which is significantly less than the typical farm in 12 other states. Still, total farm acreage is an awesome 130 million, the most of any state.

Texas has always led the nation in cotton production; that crop is still king. But the state ranks second or lower in almost every other crop, including wheat, corn, rice, and pecans, crops strongly associated with Texas. Its other number-one crops include flora such as rose bushes, lesser produce like spinach and watermelon, and occasionally a major commodity like grain sorghum.

At various times Texas farmers have produced such exotic foods as almonds, olives, papayas, guavas, quinces, avocados, and tobacco.

Alamo

No piece of Texas history is so fraught with error and exaggeration as the legend of the Alamo. The famous battle of 1836 is obviously where Texas braggadocio began. But the embellishments are unnecessary. Stripped of hyperbole, the siege and battle are just as horrifying and inspiring as the gussied-up versions most Texans prefer.

The basic facts are these: fewer than 200 Texas revolutionaries, greatly outnumbered by better-equipped Mexican soldiers, fought to the death rather than surrender—and, in the process, inflicted a serious amount of damage on the enemy. In the aftermath, American admiration and Texas pride combined to produce a story almost biblically revered but frequently full of beans.

First of all, the Alamo was not a fort but a mission, established in 1718 by Spanish missionaries from Mexico, then a Spanish possession. Its real name was the Mission San Antonio de Valero; it later came to be called the Alamo, possibly because of the cottonwood trees, or *alamos*, that grew nearby, or possibly because a group of Spanish soldiers whose hometown was Alamo de Parras had once barracked there.

Of the men in the Alamo, only a handful were native Texans; the rest came from various of the United States and six foreign countries. **David Crockett** was, of course, from the Volunteer State, Tennessee, as were **Jim Bowie** (originally) and 31 other men, the greatest number from any single place. **William Barret Travis** and James Butler Bonham, childhood friends, were both from the same small town in South Carolina. The native Texans, incidentally, were all of Mexican descent. Strictly speaking, they were not Texans at all but Mexicans, period—because Texas was then a territory owned by Mexico.

The exact number of Alamo fighters is a mystery. The most commonly cited figure is either 186 or 187. Still, noted Texas historian T. R. Fehrenbach says "150-odd," and José Enrique de la Peña, a Mexican soldier, later claimed in his memoirs that his side had counted 253 bodies of the enemy. Texans in return overestimated the number of Mexican troops. In his last letter, Travis wrote that he was "besieged, by a thousand or more of the Mexicans under Santa Anna," a number that corresponds fairly well with the 846 asserted by de la Peña, but Fehrenbach puts 4,000 in the actual battle. Estimates by rabid Texans go as high as 10,000. Dead, the Mexicans numbered around 1,600, according to most Texas sources, or 311, if you choose to believe de la Peña.

The Alamo heroes were not fighting for Texas independence. They were fighting against oppression. At the time of their death, Travis and his men were unaware that their fellow revolutionaries had reestablished the provisional government and had declared Texas a free state.

The flag that flew over the Alamo was not the Lone Star flag, which had not yet been created. Most likely the flag was, ironically, the Mexican tricolor, with "1824" emblazoned on it, representing the year of Mexico's most liberal constitution. Some historians believe the banner was that of the New Orleans Grays, but regardless, it was not a Texas flag. Mexico possesses a tattered flag that it asserts flew over the Alamo but declines to return the banner to Texas. In 1994, in fact, embarrassed Mexican officials sheepishly admitted they had *lost* the highly coveted banner.

Most popular versions of the Alamo story hold that the men were stuck inside throughout the siege. Not true. For one thing, only 145 or so men were in the Alamo when the siege began. Volunteers regularly sneaked in and out past the Mexican lines for reconnaissance. Travis dispatched messengers as well, notably his dear friend Bonham, who slipped out to seek aid and then returned, though fully aware that the Texas forces were doomed. But his mission succeeded: 32 men, all from Gonzales, arrived March 1 to reinforce the original defenders.

Any true-blooded Texan will assert hotly that every one of the heroes remained in the Alamo and that each, like Bonham, was aware of the possible consequences. In fact, one man, Louis (or Moses) Rose, deserted late in the siege after Travis admitted to his men the bleakness of the situation.

The siege, not the battle, lasted 13 days, from February 23 to March 6 (a leap year). The actual fighting lasted only an hour and a half and, despite the plethora of colorful paintings to the contrary, occurred in the darkness of predawn.

Probably the most popular anecdote in the Alamo annals is the one that depicts brave Travis drawing a line in the dirt with his sword and inviting those who were willing to die for freedom to cross the line. Naturally, as the story goes, each and every man crossed the line. Unfortunately, it *is* a story, a complete fiction, one that sprang up shortly after the fall of the Alamo and that may have derived from the deserter, Louis Rose. The line-in-the-dirt story so touched America's heart that writers immediately seized on it and embroidered it generously. The most stirring off-shoot has Bowie, laid low with typhoid fever and pneumonia, ordering that his cot be carried across the line.

Finally, there is the touchy issue of who survived the Alamo. All good Texans learned in eighth-grade Texas history class that all of the defenders, to a man, died in combat. De la Peña, though, mentioned seven survivors, including "the naturalist Davy Crockett, very well known in North America for his novel adventures." According to all versions, these seven were shortly thereafter tortured and killed, on the orders of **Santa Anna.**

Besides the surrendering seven—whether or not the story is true—there were other survivors of the Alamo; they simply were not its fighting forces. The most famous are Susannah Dickenson (whose last name is variously rendered as "Dickinson" and even "Dickerson") and her baby daughter, Angelina. Susannah's husband, Almaron, died in the battle. However, Susannah and Angelina were by no means the only ones to make it through; they were merely the only Anglo ones. The other Texan survivors have been slighted throughout history because they were Hispanic and black. There were probably 15 or so, among them one male slave, sometimes described as Travis's or Bowie's but more likely the Dickensons', and Madame Andrea Candelaria, a trained nurse who, for her services, was later awarded a pension by the State of Texas. Thus, the Alamo did indeed have its "messengers of defeat."

See also **Goliad Massacre; "Remember the Alamo!"; San Jacinto.**

Alaska

See **Biggest state.**

Alligator

To city dwellers they seem too exotic to live in Texas, but alligators have long been denizens of East and South Texas swamps. The federal government classified the American alligator as an endangered species in 1967. Since then the state's alligator population has increased tenfold, though technically it is still endangered. However, today about a dozen southeastern Texas counties, mostly coastal, allow a seasonal harvest of the alligator, with the bag limit dependent on the estimated number of the reptiles on a given landowner's property. Though there is a limited market for the skins, for most hunters the macho kick of killing a gator holds at least as much appeal as the potential profit from selling its skin.

Misinformation abounds about alligators. They rarely attack humans (the Texas Parks and Wildlife Department has never heard of such an incident in the state), though they are likely to make short work of small dogs. They do not deliberately use their tails to thwack enemies; though the flailing tail is a danger, its movement is an involuntary reflex, the result of fear and anger, and the real danger is the snapping jaws. Females as well as males bellow, probably as a territorial imperative, and both sexes avoid lying in the sun in the heat of the day.

Animal

See **Alligator; Armadillo; Buffalo; Buzzard; Camels in Texas; Cattalo; Copperhead; Coral snake; Cottonmouth; Coyote; Eagle; Horny toad; Jackalope; Jackrabbit; Javelina; Mockingbird; Mourning Dove; Mule; Mustang; Prairie dog; Pronghorn; Rattlesnake; Roadrunner; Tarantula; Woodpecker, ivory-billed.**

Annexation of Texas

Texans are justly proud of living in a state that was once an independent republic and that entered the Union by treaty, not by act of Congress. Surprise! Texas did **not** enter the Union by treaty. Though at the time of its admission the two countries were negotiating a treaty of annexation, President John Tyler, as one of his last acts in office, offered statehood under the terms of the original resolution drawn up by the House of Representatives. As a result, Texas got a better deal than it would have under the

6

treaty. For example, it became a state immediately, without having to pass through a probationary period as a mere territory.

The terms of the congressional bill included a requirement that Texas cede to the U.S. all forts, barracks, navy yards, and other property pertaining to the public defense, but it also allowed Texas to keep its public lands, a generous condition rarely found in annexation treaties. However, in exchange for that concession, Texas also had to maintain responsibility for its own public debt.

The House bill did not guarantee Texas the right to leave the Union. See **Secede, right to.**

Antelope

See **Pronghorn.**

Apollo 11

See **Armstrong, Neil.**

Armadillo

The Texas totem is not a Texan at all but an emigrant from South America. It was long confined to the Rio Grande Valley, where it has been common for close to a century, but by the thirties, after a slow northern migration, had become a frequent sight in the Hill Country and East Texas as well. (Alas, the armadillo is more often seen dead, as a road kill, than alive.) In the U.S., however, the critter is not Texas' alone. It can also be spotted in Oklahoma, Arkansas, Louisiana, and Mississippi.

The armadillo craze is not new. As long ago as 1904 curio shops offered armadillo-shell baskets for sale. (The so-called shell is really a superthick skin.) During the Depression armadillos were so often hunted for meat that locals termed them Hoover hogs. Credit for their recent popularity, though, goes largely to Austin artist Jim Franklin, whose fantastic sixties hippie-art posters indelibly linked the animal with Texas.

Miscellaneous armadillo facts: There is only one species in Texas, the nine-banded (*Dasypus novemcinctus*). All of an armadillo's litter are the same sex. Armadillos prefer to ford streams on foot, but if the water is deep enough, they *can* swim. Finally, it is true that armadillos can carry Hansen's disease, or leprosy. Some biologists shy away from saying flat out that it *is* leprosy. Because that organism cannot be cultured, they say they can't be one-hundred-percent sure. They are also uncertain if armadillos transmit the disease directly to humans, although state highway officials do acknowledge that a few of the recent leprosy cases in Texas did involve people who had handled armadillos or, in one case, eaten armadillo stew. Today, however, leprosy is treatable with antibiotics and is not the dreadful affliction it was in biblical times.

Armstrong, Neil

The first man on the moon, he told Mission Control in Houston during his 1969 steps on the lunar surface, "That's one small step for a man, one giant leap for mankind." His quote is often repeated minus the "a," which makes the statement both contradictory and redundant. In recordings of the event, static swallows up the all-important article of speech.

Armstrong's famous line was not the *first* transmission from the moon. The very first word was in fact "Houston," as in "Houston, the *Eagle* has landed."

Astrodome

Houston's Astrodome was the first domed stadium in the U.S., but today, of course, it is one of many. There are also the Superdome in New Orleans, the Kingdome in Seattle, the Silverdome in Pontiac, Michigan, the Hoosier Dome in Indianapolis, and the Hubert H. Humphrey Metrodome—also known as the Homerdome—in Minneapolis. All five are bigger than the Astrodome, which reluctantly quit promoting itself as the Eighth Wonder of the World.

Astroturf

The fake grass made famous by its use in Houston's Astrodome was not invented in Texas. Chemists at the Monsanto Company in St. Louis experimented long and hard with artificial turf before putting their final bright-green product to the test in 1966 in the 'Dome, where real grass, deprived of sunlight, had refused to grow. (The 'Dome management even tried painting the dying grass a vivid green, which didn't help a bit.) The fake turf proved so successful that the covered stadium lent the synthetic stuff its name.

Athens, Texas

The Henderson County seat was not necessarily named for the capital of Greece. Local historians are divided on the issue, some maintaining that a classics-minded matron chose the name, others that it was selected by a transplanted society lady who hailed from Athens, Georgia.

Austin, Stephen F.

The Father of Texas was not a Texan—which is logical, when you think about it. He was born in Virginia and raised in Missouri. If you want to nitpick, for part of his life he was not even an American. When he undertook the colonization of Texas, he agreed to take an oath of allegiance to Mexico, a strict requirement of that country's government.

Austin earned the sobriquet "Father of Texas" because of his determination to populate a then-wild, virtually unknown Mexican territory, but he did not at first have any interest in the project and carried on only because of his father's deathbed request that he do so. His reluctance in a way helped his mission: far from being desperate to succeed, he instigated strict rules for his colonists, kicking out men with drinking problems or unsavory reputations and therefore ending up with a rock-solid, reliable group of pioneers.

Austin's status as *empresario* did not make him powerful or rich. What monies he collected from the Mexican treasury or his colonists he usually applied to public expenses, which no one else would pay. When the colonists began chafing under Mexico's iron grip, Austin went to Mexico City to discuss their grievances and, for his trouble, was jailed for most of 1834 and 1835.

Austin did not participate in the Texas Revolution. Students of Lone Star history realize that his name is conspicuously absent from any account of the events of 1836. From January to June of that year he was in New Orleans, serving as the Republic of Texas' Commissioner to the U.S., a post to which he was appointed by the short-lived provisional government of 1835. Thus he missed the Alamo, Goliad, San Jacinto, and all the other good stuff. He died that December, having lived long enough to see his beloved Texas recognized as a republic.

Banks, distrust of

Texas' traditional suspicion of banks stems not only from the national crisis of the Great Depression in the thirties but also from the failure of its first bank ever. In 1822 the Mexican government in Texas established in San Antonio the Banco Nacional de Texas, which issued to soldiers and civil servants notes that were redeemable in gold. Shortly thereafter, though, the bigwigs in Mexico City decreed that only two-thirds of the value of the notes were to be paid in gold and the rest in paper. The bank promptly failed, and so did Texans' trust of financial institutions.

Baptist, Southern

Think Texas religion and you think Southern Baptist. But there are as many Catholics in Texas as Southern Baptists—about two and a half million each. The Catholics may be in the lead, but— Catholic churches not having quite the fervor for headcounting that Southern Baptists have—an exact tabulation is impossible.

However, if you add smaller independent groups of Baptist churches to the Southern Baptist pile, the Protestants win out after all.

See also **Religion.**

Barbecue

Texas can claim neither the word nor the style of cooking. The word derives from the Spanish *barbacoa,* and the style of cooking from Spain via the West Indies. Barbecuing has been popular in America since colonial times, and it has come to assume distinct regional differences. North and South Carolina, for example, favor pork and a sweeter sauce. Texas opts almost unrelentingly for beef and a spicy, tangy flavor.

Lyndon B. Johnson's barbecues were famous, but he was by no means the only president to throw barbecues as political events. According to social historian Stuart Berg Flexner, William Henry Harrison, while the candidate of the Whig party in 1840, hosted a Texas-size barbecue to woo voters, who consumed eighteen tons of meat. (No wonder he won the election.)

"Barbecue" can mean the food that is prepared, the grill on which it is cooked, or the event at which it is served. Alternate spellings, such as "Bar-B-Q" and "barbeque," are common but just plain wrong.

Barbed wire

It was not a Texas invention, strange as that may seem, but it owes its success to Texas.

In the 1860s and 1870s, many inventors tinkered with the idea of barbed wire, but J. F. Glidden of De Kalb, Illinois, was the first to perfect and patent. Another Yankee, John W. Gates, came to Texas to make his fortune off the newfangled spiked fencing. Arriving in San Antonio in 1876, he met with little success; ranchers scoffed at the idea of skinny little wires holding back feisty range cattle. To prove his point, Gates fenced in a herd of Longhorns in the middle of the city's Military Plaza, and though the angry cattle stormed the wire, it held easily. Texans were amazed, and Gates couldn't fill orders fast enough. His fat commissions soon earned him the nickname "Bet-a-Million." (Some sources say that "Bet-a-Million" came from his incorrigible habit of wagering huge sums on ridiculous events, such as which of two raindrops would travel more quickly down a windowpane.)

In a very real sense, barbed wire tamed Texas. Though it signaled the end of the open range, the act of chopping up Texas made the state more accessible and open to settlement and allowed ranchers to improve their stock by selectively penning and breeding cattle.

As a final note, not all Texans say "bob wahr"—unless, perhaps, a city slicker is around. It is a perfectly acceptable pronunciation, but most folks say "barb wire," omitting the "ed," much as they do in "iced tea."

Barnes, Ben

He was a political whiz kid who became a state representative at age 22, Speaker of the Texas House at 26, and lieutenant governor at 29. Many Texans associate him with the Sharpstown Scandal of 1972, in which several state officials were investigated on charges of conspiring to accept bribes in return for helping to pass controversial legislation favorable to certain banking interests. Barnes was never involved. However, his high office made him a natural target, and the media and the public eagerly linked his name to the scandal. As a result the man who had once been considered a shoo-in for the governorship came in third in the Democratic primary. Afterward he left politics for good.

Barrow, Clyde

See **Parker, Bonnie.**

Bastrop, Baron de

Felipe Enrique Neri, Baron de Bastrop, was one of early Texas' colorful cast of thousands. He was a European nobleman who used his title to sweet-talk the Mexican authorities in Texas and smooth the way for Stephen F. Austin's colonization. However, the Baron's nobility was a hoax. Though he was a member of the aristocracy, he was on the run from a charge of embezzlement in

Holland, having decided to put a goodly distance between himself and the Old World. By the time he arrived in Texas around 1805, he had prudently Hispanicized his name (he was born Philip Nering Bogel) and assumed his fictitious title. Unaware of the fraud, early Texans named a city and a county for him.

Bat wings

Two important parts of a bat, true, but also a type of wide, curved chaps favored by early cowboys. See **Chaps.**

Bean, Judge Roy

The deliberately eccentric saloonkeeper and self-styled Law West of the Pecos took to calling himself Judge before he ever was one. In 1882 the Texas Rangers appointed him a temporary justice of the peace in the tiny village of Vinegarroon, and he went on to keep the post through election. Even after he was defeated, though, he hung onto the title "Judge."

His seat of power was later Langtry, Texas, a town the Judge said he had named for the English actress Lillie Langtry, whom he greatly admired. Officials of the Southern Pacific railroad, though, asserted that well before Bean's tenure there the town had been named after a civil engineer who supervised the construction of the nearby tracks. To bolster his version, Bean christened his saloon the Jersey Lilly, after the actress's sobriquet, misspelling her name in the process.

Bean's justice was no more reliable than his word. In the time-honored style of Texas authority figures, he bent the rules to suit—or benefit—himself. He was an unblushing racist, acquitting one murderer because the victim wasn't white but Chinese, and ordering at least one Mexican to hang because he couldn't understand the defendant's Spanish. He granted divorces, an action quite beyond his legal jurisdiction, and shamelessly forced attorneys, witnesses, and spectators to buy drinks during trials in his saloon-cum-courthouse. He was also involved in sponsoring heavyweight fights, a sport then illegal in Texas. Despite his outrageous behavior, Judge Roy, more than 80 years after his death, is still Texas' best-known jurist.

Beans

See **Refried beans.**

Beef

See **Chicken-fried steak; Steak.**

Bible

To an early cowboy, the word meant not only the Good Book but also a packet of cigarette papers. To a nineteenth-century Texas Ranger, it meant the latest most-wanted list as well.

Biggest state

Texas is not, as any Alaskan will be happy to point out, and has not been since January 3, 1959, when it was toppled from its 113-year number-one spot. Alaska's admission to the Union delighted Oklahomans and Louisianans, as well as other frequent targets of Texas' superiority complex, and wounded Texas' pride worse than anything since the defeat of the Confederacy. The unkindest cut of all: the necessity of altering a line of the state song, "**Texas, Our Texas,**" from "Biggest and grandest, withstanding every test" to "Boldest and grandest," et cetera. Ouch. It still hurts.

Big Tex

The 52-foot-tall statue that greets arrivals at the annual State Fair of Texas in Dallas wasn't always a blue-jeaned, behatted cowboy. He started out life in 1949 in the town of Kerens as a giant Santa Claus during a Chamber of Commerce Christmas promotion. Three years later he was sold, made over, and adopted as the fair mascot. Big Tex wears a 75-gallon hat and size 70 boots.

Billy the Kid

Not a Texan, or even a Southerner or Westerner, he came from New York City—Brooklyn, to be exact. Texas was never much of a stomping ground for Billy, except for the Panhandle, though Texas likes to list him in its roster of outlaws, as does Hollywood.

(Texas-born World War II hero Audie Murphy played Billy in a 1950 movie proprietarily titled *The Kid From Texas*.) In 1881 he was jailed in Mesilla, New Mexico, and sentenced to death for murder, but he managed to escape. He fled to a ranch near Fort Sumner, also in New Mexico, where he was shot and killed by Sheriff **Pat Garrett** of Lincoln County, who sneaked up on him in the middle of the night—hardly a fair fight, but an accepted method of capturing a wanted criminal. The shooting made Garrett's name a household word, but the dead Billy ended up the hero. In the manner of many Western outlaws, his youth, his daring, and his reputation as a Robin Hood combined to romanticize him after his death, despite his murder of eight or more victims in cold blood.

Many sources give "William Bonney" as Billy the Kid's real name. In fact, he was born Henry McCarty and later used "Billy Antrim," taking his stepfather's surname. Not until he arrived in Lincoln County was he known as William Bonney, a name of his own choosing, though before long he was far better known as Billy the Kid.

For decades historians of the Wild West thought that Billy was left-handed. That belief arose because careless newspaper editors of the day flipped photographs of Billy, making it appear that he wore his holster on the left side.

Bird

See **Buzzard; Eagle; Mockingbird; Mourning dove; Roadrunner; Woodpecker, ivory-billed.**

Bird, State

See **Mockingbird.**

Black Bean Episode

Impressed upon every schoolchild in Texas, the black bean episode ranks up there with the Alamo as a Big Deal. The incident, however, did not occur during the Texas Revolution—though it is frequently confused with the **Goliad Massacre**—but in 1843, while

Texas was a republic. Though historical chauvinists have typically vilified the Mexicans for their cruel and summary treatment, in truth the Texans brought the trouble on themselves.

The men involved belonged to the Texas Army's Mier Expedition, a highfalutin name for what was no more than an unauthorized raiding party. (The government of Texas refused to sanction the raids or accept responsibility for the actions of the raiders.) These Texans, still irate at the depredations committed by Mexicans during the Texas Revolution, were clearly up to no good. They intended to plunder villages across the Rio Grande, to acquire livestock and generally to raise hell. When they encountered Mexican troops they cockily charged; after inflicting substantial damage, they nonetheless found themselves surrounded. Captured, the party further angered the Mexicans by escaping for a short time, but nearly all of the men—176—were recaptured. They were marched to the Mexican village of Salado, where the colonel in charge ordered that every tenth man be put to death.

Every prisoner was forced to draw a bean from a jar. White beans meant a life sentence; black beans, death. (In some versions the jar also contains brown beans, signifying torture, but that is untrue.) The 17 doomed were lined up and shot at dusk, with their more fortunate fellow captives looking on. Word of the executions filtered back to the Republic, and as a result Texas raiding parties left Mexican villages strictly alone.

Black gold

The "black" is literal but the "gold" is figurative: "black gold" is another name for oil.

Blacks

See **Slavery; Juneteenth; Poll tax; Civil War; Jordan, Barbara; Ku Klux Klan.**

Blind Man's Bluff

It's not strictly a Texan goof, but it's a misunderstanding that bears examination. The name of the game is actually "Blind

Man's Buff," the last word being a shortened form of "buffet," meaning to tap or strike, which the players take turns doing to the blindfolded victim. The confusion with "bluff" no doubt occurred because whoever is "it" tries to bluff his way into a correct guess of who touched him. In his 1982 novel, Texas writer Michael Adams used *Blind Man's Bluff* as his title, but the last word refers to a limestone cliff near the Lampasas River, a physical landmark where the novel's young protagonists hang out.

Bluebonnet

Everyone knows that the bluebonnet is not native to Texas. Well, everyone is wrong. Texas folklore has it that the seeds were either brought over by the Spanish or accidentally acquired in imports of Mediterranean grain. But in *The Texas Bluebonnet,* author Jean Andrews points out that botanists have now proven that the flower is indeed indigenous. The European bluebonnet is a different species altogether.

There are four different bluebonnets in Texas, and in 1901 one of them, *Lupinus subcarnosus,* was singled out to be the state flower. Seventy years later the Legislature okayed any other variety as well.

Bluebonnets are not always blue. Some are white, purple, or pink. Regardless of color, any single plant still counts as the state flower.

Bluebonnets were once called buffalo clover or wolf flower, and most references trace the name by which we know it today to the advent of women in Texas, who thought the shape of the bloom resembled a sunbonnet. Another possible source is a legend of the Tigua Indians, who now live in Ysleta, near El Paso. Here is their version: The tribe was plagued by a horrendous drought, and sacrifices to the spirits brought no relief. In desperation one little girl burned her favorite doll as an offering, and within days it rained. Soon after, acres of bluebonnets appeared, all the exact color of the doll's headdress.

There is one flaw in the legend, if legends can be flawed. Bluebonnets do not grow as far west as El Paso, or in climates that dry. And that is one drawback to the bluebonnet as a state flower: it does not grow statewide but proliferates only in the wetter central regions. That is also one reason that John Nance Garner, vice president for two terms under Franklin Delano Roosevelt, nominated the prickly pear as state flower when he was a state legislator at the turn of the century. Despite the prevalence of the prickly pear throughout Texas, Garner's support failed to overrule the bluebonnet, but because of his campaign Texans forever after called him Cactus Jack.

Finally, it is no longer illegal to pick bluebonnets, though the Legislature outlawed it from 1933 to 1973. (That act, now repealed, did not specify bluebonnets but covered all vegetation on state property, including highway right-of-ways.) Texans are so rabidly protective of their state symbols, though, that plucking a handful is liable to get you, if not a lynching, at least a few dirty looks.

Blue norther

A sudden, severe winter storm, it does not blow toward the north but comes from the north. And it isn't, of course, always blue; that adjective is a reference to the color of the sky as the storm swoops in, but it may be gray or black as well.

Bonham, James Butler.

See **The Alamo.**

Bonney, William

See **Billy the Kid.**

Bonnie and Clyde

See **Parker, Bonnie.**

Boundaries of Texas

The size of Texas may not appear to have changed since it joined the Union in 1845, but since then Texas has lost more than 4 million acres of land in various disputes with Mexico and the federal government. Eventually the state reclaimed 2.6 million acres, but its sheer size is still not quite as much to brag about as it once was.

In 1860 Texas arrogantly decided that its northern boundary was not merely the Red River but the north bank of the Red River and that therefore, because the river had changed course, the state owned a good chunk of what was once Oklahoma Territory. Texas christened the 1.5 million acres Greer County, promptly leased huge plots to cattle companies, and established a jail and school system. The outbreak of the Civil War prevented the U.S. from responding at the time, but in the 1880s the feds tumbled to Texas trickery and demanded the land back. Texas laughed, and the ensuing lawsuit ultimately ended up in the U.S. Supreme Court, which in 1896 determined that the U.S. was the rightful owner of Greer County. As a further slap in Texas' face, the high court ruled that the true boundary between Texas and Oklahoma was the South Fork of the Red River.

The tidelands controversy began in the forties, when the nation began to realize the value of offshore oil and gas. Most states retained mineral rights for three miles offshore, after which the U.S.'s ownership prevailed. However, Texas, the only state to enter the Union as a separate republic, had, under its terms of annexation, retained the right to three leagues of tidelands (a total of 10.4 miles), not three miles. The federal government, standing to lose millions of dollars in royalties, hotly contested the claim and, in another U.S. Supreme Court case, won. From 1948 to 1953 the feds controlled part of Texas, 2,608,774 acres of submerged Texas land in the Gulf of Mexico. Then, under pressure from many states, Congress restored the land to Texas, and though the U.S. attorney general made one more attempt to get it back, Texas prevailed and hung onto its tidelands permanently.

The Chamizal dispute was minor compared with the Greer County and tidelands cases, but it constituted an international incident. The Chamizal, between El Paso and Juárez, was the strip of land affected by the changing course of the Rio Grande. Once Mexico's, the land had lain within American jurisdiction for 99 years, causing incessant squabbling. In 1963 the two countries formally settled the dispute, and the U.S. returned 366 acres to Mexico. President Lyndon B. Johnson met the president of Mexico on the international bridge the following year to mark the end of the disagreement.

Bowie, Jim

One of the Alamo's Big Three, the Texas hero was not a Texan but a Tennessean who had lived in Louisiana and Mississippi as well. He lived in Texas only 8 of his 41 years.

Best known for his martyrdom at **the Alamo,** Bowie also left the deadly legacy of the **bowie knife,** which he did not actually design, and the tantalizing legend of a lost Spanish mine on the San Saba River, usually referred to as the Lost Bowie Mine, which supposedly contained mind-boggling masses of silver and gold. See **Buried treasure.**

Bowie knife

The preferred weapon of backwoodsmen before the advent of the sixshooter, it was popularized by **Jim Bowie,** the adventurer and Alamo hero who wielded it with consummate skill. However, Jim Bowie didn't invent the knife; he merely perfected the use of it. According to relatives, his older brother, Rezin, deserves credit for the design.

The Bowies' weapon was no piddling pocketknife, as is often assumed by the unaware. It was more akin to a butcher knife, with a wickedly curved steel blade a foot or so long and a handle heavier than most and usually of polished horn. The bowie knife was never that popular a weapon in gun-happy Texas and was better known in its era as an "Arkansas toothpick."

Brahman cattle

As the name implies, the breed originated in India, from which it was imported to Texas in the late nineteenth century. **Shanghai Pierce,** among others, championed the Brahman because it was far less susceptible than known breeds to **Texas fever.** The animal—large, placid, gray or dirty white with a fleshy, buffalo-like hump on its shoulders—is also extremely resistant to other diseases and to insects. The breed recognized in the U.S. today is a melding of as many as 30 different breeds from various regions of India, including such stalwarts as the Gir and Guzerat, which still proliferate today. Certain Brahman crosses such as Brangus (Brahman and Angus) and Braford (Brahman and Hereford) are also officially recognized as breeds in this country.

The name is correctly pronounced "BRAW-mun" or "BRAY-mun," and in South Texas, where the vast majority of the state's Brahmans live, you're apt to hear "BRAY-mer" too.

Branding

Something so immutably linked with cowboys and ranches as to seem purely Texan, the simple practice of branding livestock dates back to early Egypt, around 2000 B.C. By the fourteenth century it was common in Europe, and early Spanish explorers who trekked into Texas, such as Coronado and Cabeza de Vaca, brought along herds of branded cows. (The latter, whose name in Spanish means head of the cow, used a simple drawing of a cow's head as his brand.) The Spaniards passed on the idea to Mexican ranchers, and from them Texans adopted the practice. Branding added generously to the color of Western history and literature. Consider such famous brands as the Frying Pan and Rocking Chair and the jinglebob earmark made famous by John Chisum, who was better known as Jinglebob John. (See **Chisholm Trail.**)

Though branding conjures up a mental picture of cowboys struggling to hold down a wild-eyed cow while they apply a hot iron, the wave of the future may be cryo-branding, or branding with superchilled irons instead.

Western lore would have us believe that a brand is sacred. Actually, more than one person can use the same brand at one time. A livestock owner must register his brand with the clerk of the county where his cattle are run, but he must register a brand site as well. Most cattle are branded on the right or left hip or side. However, there are fourteen different recognized brand sites on an animal, so it is possible for fourteen different people to use the same brand, providing they burn it on in different places.

Not all ranchers use brands. Some use marks, or cuts, on various parts of the critter's anatomy, particularly earmarks, a distinctive slitting or cropping of the ear that is registered like a brand and is just as effective.

The shape as well as the position of a brand can change its official designation. For example, a plain "T" would be the T brand. But a T with an upward-slanting crossbar would be the Flying T, and the letter burned on sideways would be the Lazy T.

What cattle rustlers or "brand artists" did to disguise a pre-existing brand was called blotting. The most famous incident of blotting in Texas was the alteration of the XIT brand. See **XIT Ranch.**

Buckaroo

A cowboy, yes, but he is not so called because of bucking broncos. The word is a corruption of the Spanish *vaquero,* meaning cowboy. Few early Texans ever got the hang of pronouncing Spanish well.

Buffalo

Historians and Indians alike excoriate the white man for his deliberate slaughter of the buffalo. Once numbered in the millions, buffalo now exist in Texas only in insignificant private herds. A common misconception, though, is that the white man killed the animal for sport, wasting the valuable resource that almost singlehandedly supported the Plains tribes. Some whites undeniably shot buffalo for fun, but the majority of the beasts fell to professional hunters, who made hefty profits from the sale of the skins for buffalo robes. They often sold the flesh as well. Supplying a railroad camp with fresh meat earned Buffalo Bill Cody his nickname. Some entrepreneurs waited for the elements and the predators to do their work and then, months later, collected the bones, which were ground up for fertilizer or other commercial uses. So the whites' mass killing was not a sheerly wasteful act, as is often believed, but certainly a greedy one. Still, Indians were sickened, for they used every bit of the buffalo besides the meat and hide. The sinew provided bowstrings and thongs; the bones could be turned into tools, utensils, and ornaments; the stomachs became bags, the hooves glue, the horns magic. The fact that the demise of the buffalo led to the demise of the Indians as well as considered by the whites of the day to be a fortunate side-effect.

Perhaps because they were so easily exterminated, buffalo have the reputation of being stupid. They aren't. What made them particularly easy to kill was their poor eyesight. A hunter who approached warily enough—not allowing the wind to carry his smell, for the animals had good noses—could easily determine the lead animal in a herd and pick it off with a single shot. Deprived of their leader, the rest of the creatures milled and lowed aimlessly, allowing the marksman to take aim at leisure. Such a setup was called a stand, and some professionals claimed to have bagged as many as two hundred buffalo this way in a single day.

There is no real distinction between bison and buffalo. *Bison* is the genus name, and a bison can be not only the North American buffalo (*Bison bison*) but also the extinct prehistoric aurochs and the European wisent, both of which are also considered buffalo.

Buffalo trivia: buffalo calves have no hump, regardless of how they may be pictured.

See also **Buffalo wallows; Cattalo.**

Buffalo soldiers

Their duties had nothing to do with bison. Buffalo soldiers were black soldiers. The Comanche gave them the nickname because of their skin color and short, curly hair, which reminded the Indians of the shaggy fur on a buffalo's shoulders.

Buffalo wallow

These shallow depressions in the prairie, some still visible today, were created by buffalo rolling on their backs to scratch themselves, one of their favorite activities. A buffalo selected a nice cool spot for a wallow and then lay down and wriggled until he was covered with dirt (or, ideally but rarely, mud). The filthy coating provided protection from insects and the sun. Sometimes buffalo used the same spot over and over until a considerable hole resulted. A small band of early plainsmen in the Texas Panhandle once successfully fought off a larger group of Indians by taking shelter in a buffalo wallow.

So where's the misinformation? Well, folklore has it that a wallow is created thusly: the lead cow is on the move, her dozens or hundreds of followers dutifully trudging behind her single file. She suddenly gets an itch and quickly rolls over in the dirt to scratch the spot. Buffalo being animals of the "monkey see, monkey do" variety—so the story goes—every single buffalo in line follows her example, rolling in the very same spot and hollowing out a hell of a wallow. The idea is an erroneous one, but certainly amusing. And incidentally, buffalo traveled behind their leader not in single file but widely spread out.

Domestic cattle also enjoy a good wallow.

Buffalo wood

Early settlers' name for buffalo chips, which, when dry, made an excellent fuel in a land where true wood was scarce.

Bulldog

In Texas, the word is just as apt to be a verb than a noun. It means not only the animal but, in rodeo jargon, to trip and throw a steer by the neck, in the same way a bulldog uses his jaws to bring to down his prey.

Bull Durham

Most people recognize the name as a brand of tobacco, but few know that the name comes from a breed of cattle called Durham, better known as Shorthorn.

Bull pen

For all you nonfans of baseball, it's the place where the relief pitchers warm up in a ballpark. (It can also mean the pitchers themselves.) The most obvious explanation of the name is that the enclosure resembles a pen for bulls. Alternately, the word means a jail or cell, because in the nineteenth century policemen were called bulls. For a third version, one with a Texas twist, here's this: Early ballparks often featured billboards advertising **Bull Durham** tobacco, the most popular tobacco of its day. In Austin, one story goes, the Bull Durham sign was right next to the area where the pitchers warmed up. Thus was born the term "bull pen," which spread nationwide.

Buried treasure

Texas folklore abounds with stories of buried treasure. Most of them involve gold, silver, and murder but few hard facts. Still, who is to say the tales aren't true?

Possibly the most famous tale of buried treasure is that associated with Texas hero **Jim Bowie.** According to the story, before his ill-fated participation in the siege of the Alamo, Bowie either hid or learned the location of a huge treasure somewhere in the vicinity of Llano, Mason, or Menard counties. The loot ranges anywhere from three muleloads of silver to the fabulously rich Lost Bowie Mine to a cave full of gold, depending on which version you choose.

Another treasure tale is tied to the unfortunate Emperor Maximilian of Mexico, whose personal fortune of gold, silver, and jewels may languish somewhere below the surface of Pecos County. Supposedly the guards he sent to protect and hide his treasure held up the wagon train themselves and secreted the loot in a spot they could never again find.

The Texas Revolution yielded two tantalizing tales of treasure. One has it that while fleeing the Battle of San Jacinto, Mexican soldiers pushed into the Neches River a cannon packed breech to muzzle with gold coins, successfully hiding the money from the attacking Texans. Another tale alleges that the pay chests for Santa Anna's troops are buried somewhere in a South Texas bog. After the Mexican Army surrendered, they were never found.

One more missing treasure trove is that of the Singer family, pro-Union sympathizers who were forced to leave Confederate Texas because of the Civil War. They left $80,000 in gold on Padre Island, but when they returned after the war, the island had been ravaged by a hurricane and the hiding place forever obscured.

Burrito

The origin of the name is hazy, but it evolved perhaps because the flour tortilla rolled around the meat or bean filling resembles a fat little burro. Then again, it could pertain to the frequently unidentifiable nature of the meat.

Many Texans consider the burrito a standby of Tex-Mex cooking, but it is genuinely Mexican, as is the flour tortilla. According to Diana Kennedy, a longtime authority on Mexican food, both are popular all across the northern Mexican states. Their proximity to the border accounts for their popularity in Texas.

See also **Chili; Fajita.**

Burro

See **Mule.**

Bush, George

The former president is not a native Texan. George Herbert Walker Bush was born in Connecticut (where his father, Prescott Bush, was a longtime U.S. senator). However, he did live in Texas for almost 18 years. The prep-school and Yale University graduate moved to Midland in 1950, and with a friend founded Zapata Petroleum. His plunge into the then-booming oil business soon produced a sizable fortune, which funded his entry into Texas politics. In 1959 Bush moved to Houston, where he twice ran unsuccessfully for a U.S. Senate seat. He did, however, serve two terms in the U.S. House of Representatives, and went on to serve as ambassador to the United Nations and director of the Central Intelligence Agency before serving as Ronald Reagan's vice-president and, in 1988, winning the office of chief executive for himself.

Bush's oldest son, George W., was also born in Connecticut, though he has lived the majority of his life in Texas. Clearly his birthplace made no difference to the Texans who overwhelmingly elected him governor in 1994. That makes him only the third Republican governor in Texas history, after Reconstruction appointee E. J. Davis and 1978 winner William P. Clements.

Bush, George W.

See **Bush, George.**

Butte

See **Mesa.**

Buzzard

Though any legitimate Texan uses "buzzard" to describe that big ugly bald thing feasting on highway carrion, serious birders frown on the term. They use "turkey vulture," which is ornithologically correct. The distinction is important because in England a buzzard is a kind of hawk, which is a far different critter from a vulture (though the two share the same order, Falconiformes).

Buzzards—er, turkey vultures—are probably the most frequently sighted birds in Texas, as well as the most often disliked, being something of a feathered version of the Grim Reaper. Many people assume they carry disease, but in fact they more often prevent it. As scavengers they serve as Nature's garbagemen, removing rotting carcasses from roads and fields. So, do not despise the buzzard his place in the scheme of things—unless the scheme of things is directly over your barn.

Cabeza de Vaca

One of the first European explorers in the New World, Cabeza de Vaca traveled all the way from southeastern Texas to Mexico City on foot. But he certainly didn't mean to. Part of a Spanish expedition intended to colonize the Gulf Coast, he was shipwrecked about 1528 on what most historians think was Galveston Island, though possibly it was a different Texas island or even one off Louisiana. Only he and a few companions survived the trek across Texas, an eight-year nightmare of bad weather, meager food, and hostile Indians. Arriving in Mexico at last, he told, besides his own incredible story, that of the fabulous Seven Cities of Cibola. (See **Cibola, Seven Cities of.**)

Cabeza de Vaca's name is often confused. His last name was not "Vaca" but "Cabeza de Vaca." However, "Cabeza de Vaca"—which means "head of the cow"—was the name of his mother's family, not his father's. He preferred the matronymic because it conveyed higher social status than his father's name, Alvar Núñez.

Cactus

Rare is the native Texan who has not run afoul of the prickly pear, the state's most common cactus. There are actually several species of the prickly pear, all of which are prickly but none of which has anything to do with a pear. The pads are roughly the color and shape of a pear, perhaps, but the cactus' fruit tastes nothing like it. Mexicans call the plant *higo chumba,* "Indian fig." The small pink to purple fruits—called *tunas*—are loaded with seeds and—unlike the pads, which advertise their danger—are covered with tiny, almost invisible spines that spell woe to the ungloved picker. If a determined soul can get past the spines and the seeds, though, the tunas make a delicious jelly. The pads, plucked and peeled, are called *nopales* and eaten as a vegetable or in salads.

In 1901 John Nance Garner favored the prickly pear blossom as state flower, thus earning the nickname "Cactus Jack." (See **Bluebonnet.**)

Another cactus myth involves barrel cacti, which are actually quite uncommon in Texas. Barrel cacti are reputed to contain enough clear, fresh water to save the life of a thirsty desert dweller. Untrue. Sliced open, a plant yields a mouthful or two of slimy, damp pulp, which, if you're really that parched, might do the trick. On the whole, though, it's a terrible waste of a rare cactus.

Three types of Texas cactus recognizable even to most city folks are ocotillo, yucca, and agave, the century plant. However, none of the trio is, botanically speaking, a cactus. Ocotillo has tiny leaves and true thorns, unlike the succulents. Yucca is a member of the lily family, and the century plant is an amaryllis. It actually blooms more often than once a century, despite the implication of its name, and sometimes as often as every 15 years.

See also **Saguaro.**

Calaboose

The slang term for tail is a corruption of the Spanish word *calabozo* meaning prison or dungeon. A popular term with cowboys, it actually predates Western usage by a couple of decades. Harriet

Beecher Stowe, for example, used the word in her 1852 novel, *Uncle Tom's Cabin*.

Calf fries

See **Mountain oysters.**

Calico

Not only a cotton fabric or a multicolored cat but also, to early cowboys, a pinto horse or any variety, human or animal, of female.

Camels in Texas

The U.S. Army's importation and use of camels in Texas is a well-known and deservedly funny footnote in the state's history. But history regards the camel experiment as a failure, when in fact it succeeded. Thirty-three of the ungainly and odoriferous creatures arrived at Indianola in 1856, followed by a second batch of 41. Because they could fare so well without water, the Army assigned them to duty in West Texas. Eventually the experiment foundered—but not because of the camels, who proved themselves adept at tracking Indians and transporting supplies. Horse-loving Texans were simply not pro-camel, and besides, the outbreak of the Civil War moved camels way down the Army's list of priorities. Thus the camels were sold or relegated to use in pack trains. Proving the stamina of its species, at least one animal escaped and lived happily for years in West Texas. Travelers and residents reported sightings of the beast off and on for twenty more years after the war.

Camino Real

The King's Highway or Royal Road, established by the Spanish in the early nineteenth century, ran from Nacogdoches to San Antonio. The king never used it, of course; the title was merely a courtesy. Nor was it a highway at all; it was more of a path, rutted, overgrown, sometimes barely traceable on the prairie.

Like many modern highways, the Camino Real had a high death toll, but not because of vehicular accidents. Indians, under-

31

standably hostile, lurked about the frontage road, and there were no Dairy Queens, Minor Emergency Centers, or Best Westerns to offset hunger, thirst, and fatigue.

Canadian River

The name has nothing to do with Canada. It comes from the Spanish *cañada*, meaning either a gully or cattle path. Another cowboy corruption.

Capital of Texas

Austin has never been the *only* capital of Texas. It has, however, always been the only capital of the State of Texas.

When Texas belonged to Spain, its territorial capitals included, in about 1721, Los Adaes (a site now in Louisiana) and, 50 years later, San Antonio. When Spain acknowledged Mexico's independence in 1821, the capital became Saltillo, in Coahuila, and nine years later Monclova in the same Mexican state.

The nervous new Republic of Texas changed its capital eight times in just over four years, starting with San Felipe de Austin and then switching in turn to Washington-on-the-Brazos, Harrisburg, Galveston Island, Velasco, Columbia, Houston, and finally Waterloo, which was renamed Austin after Stephen F.

Besides those 12 places, a picky person could add the capitals of the five nations other than the Republic that once ruled Texas: Madrid, Paris, Mexico City, Washington, D.C., and the two capitals of the Confederate States of America—Richmond, Virginia, and Montgomery, Alabama. That makes a grand total of 18 different capital cities.

Capitol

See **State Capitol.**

Carthage, Texas

The name of the East Texas city brings to mind ancient Carthage, now part of Africa, but the town was really named for Carthage, Mississippi.

Catholicism

See **Baptist, Southern; Religion.**

Cattalo

Not merely a cross between cattle and buffalo. Legendary cow-man Charles Goodnight, the first Texan to attempt serious cross-breeding, specified that cattalo were the offspring of buffalo bulls and domestic cows. Because that cross caused difficult births and also produced many sterile males, however, it was eventually abandoned, and today the few cattalo that are raised are second or third generation crossed back on domestic cows. They are also called Beefalo.

Cattle

Texas is the nation's largest producer of cattle, with 13.6 million head in 1992—nearly all of which were beef breeds (as opposed to the dairy varieties). But that number pales beside the total raised in India: a staggering 271.4 million head. Of course, in that Hindu nation, the cow is more likely to be venerated than incinerated.

See also **Brahman cattle; Branding; Hereford; Longhorn; Okie; Santa Gertrudis; Trail drive.**

Cattle guard

It doesn't guard cattle—it guards against them. Cattle are naturally chicken, so to speak, and because cattle guards brandish the double threat of tripping and falling, cattle shy away from them. Cattle guards provide an ingenious way to keep herds separate (and also to protect crops) without forcing a cowboy, farmer, or other wayfarer to stop to open and close numerous gates. More proof of the low level of the bovine brain: Once cattle have become accustomed to the presence of a cattle guard, a fake one will contain them just as well. Cattle won't even cross the shadow of a cattle guard, or anything similarly striped on the ground.

In Canada cattle guards are called Texas gates.

Century plant

Not a type of cactus but a relative of the amaryllis. It blooms much more often than every century—sometimes even every fifteen years. See **Cactus.**

Chamizal dispute

See **Boundaries of Texas.**

Chaps

The protective leggings worn by cowboys prevent chapping, no doubt, but they get their name from the equivalent Mexican garment called *chaparreras*, leggings to wear in the chaparral. Chaps are not trousers—they are worn *over* trousers—and they are made of leather, not the fluffy white sheepskin often portrayed in books and movies. The word is correctly pronounced "shaps."

Chicken-fried steak

Nothing makes a Texan start to salivate faster than a tender, juicy slab of chicken-fried steak swimming in cream gravy. But originally steak was chicken-fried—that is, dipped in batter and prepared like fried chicken—because it wasn't tender or juicy at all. Range cattle usually yielded tough, even stringy beef, and ranch cooks and farm wives took to frying the bejesus out of it to soften it up. The cream gravy helped return some of the flavor that the prolonged cooking removed. But it was still a tasty dish, and today's CFS, prepared with grain-fed beef, is better yet. Not necessarily good *for* you—but good nonetheless.

Chihuahua

The most popular toy dog in the U.S., the pint-size pup hails from Mexico, where the ancient Toltec culture immortalized the breed in carvings a thousand years ago. The name comes from the state of Chihuahua, but the depictions of the dog also appear in ancient buildings and stone art in the Mexican states of Yucatán and Puebla as well, so more than one region of that country can claim to have spawned the wee critter's forebears. Chihuahuas, which generally weigh one to six pounds, are beloved as pets today, but at one time they may have been used as food. In an 1878 Kennel Club show in New York, one entrant, most likely a Chihuahua, was labeled a "Chinese Edible Dog," after another country that has historically enjoyed canine cuisine.

Chihuahuas, by the way, are a different breed than the Mexican hairless.

Chili

Not authentic Mexican food but pure Texan. The rise of chili, named Texas' state dish in 1977, began in the 1880s in San Antonio, where at dusk enterprising women set up tables and stoves in downtown's Military Plaza and offered irresistibly delicious bowls of a meat stew that was equally hot in temperature and spice. The chili queens provided a lively and distinctive atmosphere that made San Antonio's night life and street life unmatched by any other place in Texas.

The craze for chili rapidly spread across the state, eventually leading to the founding of Texas' Gebhardt and Wolf Brand labels, giants of the canned-chili industry.

Public health officials closed down the chili stands in 1936, and from then on Dallas took over as the chili capital of Texas. In the fifties Dallasites founded the Chili Appreciation Society, and Frank X. Tolbert of that city, Texas' original chili expert, popularized the phrase "bowl of red."

"Chili" is the correct spelling for the combination of meat, peppers, and spice. "Chile" means pepper (the vegetable, not the spice), and usually a hot pepper to boot. *Chile con carne* originally meant peppers stewed with meat, though now it is widely considered the same thing as chili.

Beans are completely unacceptable in Texas chili, and tomatoes are almost as verboten. So are bell peppers, celery, bulgur, and various other greenery and grains added by Yankees or vegetarians. However, many Texans might be surprised to learn that much authentic chili contains *masa harina*, the fine-grained cornmeal used to make tortillas; the *masa* serves to bind and thicken the chili without affecting the taste. True Texas chili is usually made of beef; variations include venison, rabbit, or ostrich, but never pork.

See also **Burrito; Fajita.**

Chisholm Trail

The most famous trail in the West was the Chisholm Trail, a name even Yankees recognize. But the man for whom it was named never drove a single cow up it. Jesse Chisholm was an Indian trader who, by 1865, had traveled so frequently through Indian territory (from what is now Wichita, Kansas, south through Oklahoma to the Red River) that his well-worn wagon tracks inevitably became the route followed north by cattlemen. Eventually the trail became so popular with drivers that it extended all the way through Texas to the Rio Grande; dozens of spur trails branched off from it in all directions.

Some residents of Paris, Texas, always disputed the naming of the original Chisholm Trail. They maintained that it was properly spelled "Chisum" and was named for local pioneering cowman John Chisum, also known as Jinglebob John, after his ranch and earmark. (See **Branding.**) John Chisum was without a doubt one of the first Texans to drive cattle, sending his first herd with another equally famous cowman, Charles Goodnight, in 1866, a date only one year later than Jesse Chisholm could claim. However, the route of Chisum's cattle stretched from Texas to New Mexico, not Kansas, and was better known as the Goodnight-Loving Trail. Sorry, Jinglebob John.

Christmas tree

Not just a seasonal decoration, to an oil worker it is also the elaborate network of control valves and pressure gauges mounted atop a completed well to regulate the flow of oil or gas.

Cibola, Seven Cities of

One of the earliest and finest examples of Texas brag. A spin-off of the fabulous tale of El Dorado ("The Golden One")—a myth that persistently captured the imagination of Spanish conquistadores—the Seven Cities of Cibola supposedly combined to create an Indian metropolis with streets of silver and houses of gold, whose inhabitants staggered under the weight of their jewels. **Cabeza de Vaca** heard tales of the mythical Cibola as he struggled across Texas, retelling them to an eager audience when he arrived in Mexico City in 1536. In 1540, Francisco Vásquez de Coronado set out after the Seven Cities, guided and abetted by a mendacious friar whom he sent home in disgrace after the legendary cities of gold turned out to be a cluster of pueblos belonging to the cliff-dwelling Indians of present-day western New Mexico. Still gullible, though, Coronado bit again, setting out the next year for the equally splendid Gran Quivira, which supposedly lay somewhere in what is now the Texas Panhandle. Disappointed again, he returned to face disgrace himself and was fined and penalized for neglecting his home duties in favor of a wild-goose chase.

Civil War

Though the War Between the States inevitably altered the course of Texas history, it actually affected Texas much less than it did the rest of the South. For one thing, Texas' culture has never been purely Southern but has always been a combination of Western and Southern tradition, and the state shared little with the rest of the Confederacy besides its traditional sanction of slavery and an economic dependence on King Cotton. In fact, about a third of Texas' population, including **Sam Houston,** opposed secession.

In addition, geography saved Texas from most of the war's depredations. The state was too far away for the Yankee infantry to overrun it, so most Texans never saw a Union soldier throughout the war, unless he was a P.O.W. Much of Texas never felt the sting of the Civil War at all; in some parts of the state there were other, more pressing matters, such as border disputes and raids along the Rio Grande and attacks by and against Indians in the Panhandle and West Texas. The Union Army did, however, occupy El Paso for three years to establish a barrier to Confederate infiltration of California. Also, for short periods, the Union Navy held Galveston and Sabine Pass and successfully disrupted the shipping of Texas cotton.

Texas as a whole suffered mainly because of inflation and shortages of food and supplies, and because at least fifty thousand and maybe as many as ninety thousand of its menfolk forsook their farms and ranches to serve in the rebel army. However, unlike the true Southern states, Texas had a sizable contingent of Northern sympathizers. At least two thousand Texans, including many German settlers and freed blacks, left the state to join up with the North.

Because Texas missed out on most of the color and drama of the Civil War (or was spared from it, depending on how you look at it), the state has always been proud that the last shots fired in the war were on Texas soil, on May 11, 1865, at the battle of Palmito Ranch near Brownsville, where, supposedly, a handful of tough Texas soldiers decided they would never say die. Alas, the truth is less dramatic. The skirmish occurred not because the Confederates refused to give up but because they had not yet received news of Robert E. Lee's surrender a month earlier. Seeing the approaching Yankee soldiers, they had no choice but to fire. So strictly speaking, the war was over when the Confederates won at Palmito Ranch, killing 30 of the already victorious Yanks.

Another never-say-die attitude is associated with General **Edmund Kirby-Smith** (often called Kirby Smith, though "Kirby" was not his first name but rather part of his last name; he adopted the hyphenation to distinguish himself from the multitudinous other Southern Smiths). Kirby-Smith was the last Confederate officer to surrender his command, hanging in there until June 2, 1865, almost two months after Appomattox, when he finally packed it in in Galveston. His delayed surrender, though, was a defiant gesture on his part only. By the time he gave up, nearly all his soldiers had already deserted him.

In many ways Texas suffered more during Reconstruction than during the war. Union soldiers, almost unknown in the state during the actual hostilities, occupied much of postwar Texas, and hostile feelings ran high. Local and state governments were ineffective or nonexistent. Border raids and Indian wars raged unchecked, and to the horror of many Texans, the slaves had been freed.

A final bit of Civil War misinformation needs clearing up: Texas was not officially readmitted to the Union in 1865, when the war ended. Reconstruction and **martial law** ended in 1870, at which time Texas, and the rest of the South, again became part of the United States.

Cliburn, Van

Although many Texans assume the much-honored pianist has a two-word last name, Van (short for Lavan) is his middle name and Cliburn his last. (First name: Harvey.) The Kilgore native, winner of the prestigious Tchaikovsky piano competition in 1958, did much to convince the rest of the nation that Texas not only understood but could actually produce and even advance culture.

Cohabitation

Though prevalent today, to the horror of the religious right and other conservative individuals, living together has long been a Texas tradition. When Texas belonged to Mexico in the 1820s and 1830s, Roman Catholicism was a condition of colonization, although few priests were available to travel the huge territory administering the rite of matrimony. (See **Religion.**) Thus couples in love simply agreed to get married someday and then moved in together while they waited for a cleric to come by and make it official. (When a priest did show up, he often conducted huge mass ceremonies.) Just as often, though, the lovers had a falling-out and simply dissolved their agreement without bothering about its legality.

Today cohabitation by two people who hold themselves out to be married and consider themselves married constitutes marriage under Texas law.

Colorado Kool-Aid

Not a soft drink but a beer. Coors acquired the nickname because of its reputation as a wimpy, watery beer—at least in the opinion of macho Texas beer-guzzlers—though its alcohol content is not significantly different from more putatively manly brands.

Colorado River

The name has nothing to do with the state of Colorado. "Colorado" means "colored" in Spanish and carries the connotation of "colored red." Hence, at least in the beginning, the name most likely referred to the river's color. The Colorado River's water is quite clear, however. It's possible that the early Spaniards in Texas confused the Colorado with the nearby Brazos, whose waters can be reddish on occasion, or that Spanish mapmakers accidentally transposed the two names. The Red River, indisputably named for its hue, is another story entirely.

Colt .45

No gun is more famous than the Colt .45. The very name conjures up images of fierce Rangers, fleeing Indians, brave cowboys, and flinty-eyed gunslingers. The Colt .45 is unquestionably the most famous revolver ever, but despite the romantic ring of its name, the .45-caliber models were not the most important Colts. And though the gun, better known as the six-shooter, played a major role in the taming of Texas, it was not invented by a Texan at all.

Samuel Colt of Paterson, New Jersey, first had the brainstorm: a pistol with a revolving chamber, one that could shoot six times without reloading. In 1838 he produced his first model, a .34 caliber, which, in a flash of intuition, he called the Texas. Unfortunately, there was no need in the East for such a pistol, but the few that made their way to Texas galvanized the Rangers there. A six-gun was exactly what they needed to tip the scales of the Indian wars in their favor.

Up to New Jersey headed Ranger Captain Samuel Walker. There, to the delight of Samuel Colt, he tracked down the young inventor and discussed with him improvements on the basic design. From the tête-à-tête came the Walker-Colt, any Ranger's pride and joy, a big, heavy gun designed for a man astride, with a larger caliber of .44. Despite the gun's popularity in Texas, though, Samuel Colt went bankrupt; the limited demand wasn't enough to keep him afloat. A few years later, during the Mexican War, he got another chance: a government contract for his revolver. He was back in business.

His most famous gun of all was the 1873 model, the Peacemaker. This was the legendary Colt .45, though shortly after its introduction Colt's company switched to a .44-caliber version. Still, it went down in history as the Colt .45, and the company sold about 350,000 of them. Of the gun that won the West, Texans said, "God made some men big and some men small, but Sam Colt made them all equal."

Despite its lasting fame, the Colt .45 probably was not the most popular gun in Western history. That would undoubtedly be the Winchester repeating rifle, owned and used not only by cowboys but also by farmers, miners, and almost every other resident of the West.

Come and Take It

A provocative slogan of the Texas Revolution, it was imprinted upon a banner flown during the battle at Gonzales in October 1835. The "it" does not refer to the flag, however, but to a cannon with which the Texans had been regularly peppering the enemy. The cannon was not even Texas'. The Mexicans had originally given the cannon to Gonzales several years before to strengthen the town's defenses against Indians, and they were none too happy at having their own weapon turned against them.

Community property

Texas is one of eight community property states, which share the principle but enact it with greatly varying laws. For example,

California is referred to as a community property state, but it commonly awards alimony as part of divorce decrees, whereas in Texas a spouse cannot be forced to pay alimony to his or her ex.

The basic notion underlying Texas community property law is that each spouse has a claim on the property or assets earned, purchased, or acquired *during* the marriage. Therefore there is no great advantage to marrying someone who amassed his or her wealth before tying the knot. Contrary to popular belief, it makes no difference whose name is on the paycheck, car title, or deed to the house. Naturally there are a few exceptions just to make things interesting; for example, gifts and inheritances are not community property but separate property.

In Texas, community property law is most often invoked in divorce cases. Despite a widespread misconception, community property is rarely split fifty-fifty. The court takes into account each spouse's earning potential, abilities, training, and other factors. A judge may award a long-suffering wife who has put her ex through medical school ninety percent of the community estate, recognizing and rewarding her contribution to his education. For his part, the husband can't complain; after the divorce she can make no further financial claim on him, so his future income is his alone.

Child support is an issue considered apart from community property.

Confederacy

See **Civil War.**

Confederate Air Force

Of the CAF's 135 planes, none flew for the Confederacy during the Civil War. But you knew that, didn't you? The name Confederate Air Force began as a joke, after an anonymous prankster painted the phrase on the fuselage of one of the elderly aircraft. All of the aircraft in the flying museum adjacent to the Midland-Odessa airport are vintage World War II. They are referred to en masse as the Ghost Squadron. Despite their age, more than half are in flying condition at any given time. The rest are being repaired or restored by the organization's confederacy of plane fanciers. CAF top brass is Colonel Jethro E. Culpepper, who is about as legitimate as a Civil War-era plane, and all regular members of the CAF are colonels as well.

Copperhead

This poisonous pit viper is common in much of Texas. There are three subspecies in the state. However, the copperhead is in fact rarely deadly. Its poison is relatively mild compared with that of the **coral snake** or **rattlesnake,** and it is often confused with the harmless eastern hognose snake, which resembles it in coloring.

The word "copperhead" also means a resident of the North who, during the Civil War, sympathized with the South.

See also **Cottonmouth; Snakebite.**

Coral snake

Looks are deceiving when you're talking about the colorful Texas coral snake. Slender and pretty, the coral snake has thick bands of red and black divided by thin yellow rings, and it is the deadliest reptile in North America. But because it is not a pit viper, it is responsible for very few reported snakebites and even fewer deaths. Its shorter, blunter fangs make envenomation difficult.

Coral snakes are often confused with king snakes, milk snakes, or scarlet snakes, all of which have some combination of red, black, or yellow bands. The coral snake alone, however, has its red and yellow bands next to each other (though in the Texas Longnose snake, bits, not bands, of red and yellow may touch). The simple rhyme "Red and yellow, kill a fellow; red and black, friend of Jack"—or some variety thereof—makes identifying the dangerous coral snake a little easier.

See also **Copperhead; Cottonmouth; Rattlesnake; Snakebite.**

Corbitt, Helen

The mentor of thousands of Texas cooks and chefs, she showed the state and the rest of the nation that Lone Star cooking could legitimately be called cuisine. But Helen Corbitt was not a native Texan; she was a New Yorker who had taught at the University of Texas and later moved up through positions at country clubs and hotel dining rooms to Neiman-Marcus in Dallas, where in 1955 she began to operate the classy store's Zodiac Room and produce Texas classics like **Texas caviar** and **prairie fire.**

Corn

See **Agriculture.**

Cortinas, Juan

A border bandit who preceded **Pancho Villa** by fifty years, Juan Cortinas (sometimes called Cortina) has always been much in Villa's shadow. But Cortinas was a greater threat to Texas than Villa ever was.

Cortinas called his bloodthirsty group of followers his army, and waged war against the Texas side of the Rio Grande Valley. Whereas Pancho Villa invaded Columbus, New Mexico—a foolhardy move that is often erroneously considered the only foreign invasion of U.S. soil—Juan Cortinas not only invaded but also terrorized and laid siege to Brownsville in September 1859. He entered the town to free Mexican prisoners held in the jail, killing four Texans in the process, then moved himself and his men into the Fort Brown barracks, which, to Brownsville's misfortune, the U.S. Army had recently abandoned. Later retiring to a ranch outside town (which his highborn mother had inherited), he controlled all routes in and out of the town for a month, repulsing a weak civil guard that tried to chase him off. A couple of weeks later he bested a force of Texas Rangers who also tried to oust him. Cortinas was not overcome until late in December, when the U.S. Army, acting at last, marched to reoccupy Fort Brown and then to battle Cortinas, killing 60 of his men and successfully routing him.

Despite Cortinas' ultimate defeat, his prestige was so great that he went on to become governor of the Mexican state of Tamaulipas—where he was born, though he always claimed Texas citizenship.

Cotton

See **Agriculture.**

Cottonmouth

Properly termed the western cottonmouth, the snake gets its common name from the white interior of its mouth—which it stretches frighteningly wide as a threat—and not because it has anything to do with cotton. There is not enough water near cotton fields to attract cottonmouths, which like to hang out around swamps and lakes.

A popular story that has become almost a modern legend involves a nameless Texas water skier who, while enjoying his favorite sport, takes a spill into a wriggling nest of baby cottonmouths and dies in agony from hundreds of bites. The story is bunk, for most cottonmouths bear only half a dozen young at a time, and though the snakes like water they bear their young on land.

See also **Copperhead; Coral snake; Rattlesnake; Snakebite.**

Cottontail

See **Jackrabbit.**

Cowboy

Since the Civil War the term has meant a man who works with cattle. However, the word has existed for much longer than that. In England in the early eighteenth century, a cowboy was a youngster who herded cattle, and during the American Revolution the name "Cowboys" was contemptuously applied to a group of Tory guerrillas in Westchester County, New York, probably because of their crude tactics in dealing with their foes. In the days of the Republic of Texas, the name was adopted by a group of hell-raisers under the leadership of Ewen Cameron, who subjected Mexico to a series of thieving raids. (See **Black Bean Episode.**) By the 1880s the word "cowboy" was well-known and widely used across America. Subsequently "cowman" also arose; the difference between the two terms was wealth. The cowman owned the cattle and the land; the cowboy worked for him.

Few words are as suggestive and romantic as "cowboy." The cowboy's influence was so great that a hundred years after his heyday, his imprint on the state still remains. But only a tiny percentage of Texans were ever cowboys—and of those, even fewer actually participated in the short-lived phenomenon of the trail drive. The average Texas man was much more likely to be a farmer than a cowboy, and certainly farmers, especially cotton farmers, were a much greater factor in the state's economy than cowboys ever were.

Hollywood portrayals to the contrary, most cowboys, particularly those participating in trail drives, were quite young, in their teens or early twenties.

Cow chip

Lest visitors and transplanted Texans be misinformed, cow chips are not a snack food. They are dried cow dung. Fresh, a unit of the substance is known as a cow pie, a cow patty, or even a meadow muffin. Bullshit, however, is quite a different thing.

Coyote

Coyotes really do howl at the moon, but they will also howl at any other bright light out of sheer curiosity. As a general rule, though, coyotes are much more likely to yap than howl, and they often carry on long-distance conversations with other coyotes, much like the midnight bark in Disney's *101 Dalmatians*.

The coyote has an undeserved reputation as a coward, mostly because it combines the natural shyness of most wildlife with the habit of running away with its tail between its legs.

Both "KYE-ote" and "kye-OH-tee" are acceptable pronunciations.

Criminal

See **Billy the Kid; Cortinas, Juan; Davis, Cullen; Hardin, John Wesley; Hill, Dr. John; Kennedy, John F., assassination of; Mossler, Candace; Parker, Bonnie; Starr, Belle; Villa, Pancho.**

Crockett, David

The best-known hero of the Alamo, Davy was a man of myths. First of all, Davy apparently rarely wore a coonskin cap, though the idea of him without one is like Old Glory without its stars. Though tall, he was a little pudgy, not too handsome, and definitely middle-aged (49 at the time of the siege)—details frequently omitted in movies and on TV. His beloved trusty rifle, Old Betsy, was left behind in Tennessee when he came to Texas to fight in the Alamo; so much for depictions of him brandishing it at the pesky Mexicans. And despite the much-loved Disney theme song labeling him "King of the Wild Frontier," he wasn't born on a mountaintop but merely in the mountainous country of northeastern Tennessee. Whether or not he really killed a bear when he was only three will never be known, so let's give him the benefit of the doubt.

But the big question about Davy is whether he really died at the Alamo. Any loyal Texan flinches at the thought, and yet apparently seven of the defenders survived the slaughter, only to be tortured and killed by their Mexican captors. A Mexican officer, José Enrique de la Peña, in a diary unpublished until 1955, identified Crockett by name as one of the seven Texas soldiers who survived. A Texas sergeant, George M. Dolson, also asserted in a letter published in late 1836 that a Mexican soldier for whom he served as interpreter also swore that Crockett survived the battle. Such a revelation is shocking, and yet once upon a time folks had to forgo their preconceived notions and accept the fact that the earth was round.

See also **Alamo.**

Crop

See **Agriculture.**

Cyclone

Now used—though rarely—in Texas to mean a tornado, a hundred years ago the word signified a hurricane. See **Tornado; Weather.**

Dallas

The granddaddy of prime-time soaps, which ran from 1978 to 1991, was set in Texas but filmed in California. However, the opening credits unscrolled over legitimate Texas footage of oil wells, Hereford cattle, and wheat fields. The exterior shots of the Ewing family mansion, Southfork, were of a real Texas home near Dallas, and some incidental scenes were shot on location in Dallas skyscrapers and other buildings.

Davis, Cullen

No matter what Texans at large may think, the Fort Worth multimillionaire was acquitted of murder. Prosecutors argued that Davis, disguised entirely in black, had surprised his estranged wife, Priscilla, late on an August night in 1976 as she returned from an evening out with her lover, Stan Farr, to the ritzy Davis mansion in a fashionable section of the city. The man in black shot Priscilla in the chest, but she managed to run away. Farr, hit four times, died instantly. Summoned to the mansion, police discovered, in the basement, the body of Priscilla's twelve-year-old daughter. She also had been shot to death.

The murder case had all the elements needed to make headlines across Texas: a gun, a sexy blonde, a millionaire. Davis was tried in the media and, in the minds of his fellow Texans, found guilty, but he prevailed in court, aided by the flashy and effective representation of Houston attorney **Racehorse Haynes.**

Two years later, Davis was again arrested, charged with having hired a hit man to kill the judge who was presiding over the bitter divorce proceedings between Cullen and Priscilla. Again he was represented by Racehorse Haynes, and this time the case ended in a mistrial.

Deer

You can't tell the age of a buck from the number of points on his antlers, just as you can't tell the age of a rattlesnake from the number of rings on his rattle. Also, it is not necessarily illegal to shoot a doe. After extensive surveying of the deer population, the Texas Parks and Wildlife Department sets the number of deer, male and female, that can be harvested each year in each county. Most deer killed are whitetail; a small percentage are mule.

Desert

Despite the stereotyped image of Texas—even among those who know better—as a vast, arid wasteland complete with cow skulls and cactus, surprisingly little of Texas is true desert. Plains and prairies do not count, no matter what city folks might think. The only legitimate candidate is the Chihuahuan Desert, which in Texas falls within the Trans-Pecos, a region of about 18 million acres west of the Pecos River that forms the western corner of Texas. Thus Texas' desert is actually less than ten percent of the state's total land area—whereas some fifteen percent is woodland, a far less popular or believable image.

Dixie

Something Texas is not part of. "Dixie" means the Southern states, and Texas has never been strictly Southern. It is equally Western—perhaps more so. Though Texas was a slave state and fought for the Confederacy in the **Civil War,** it never had the entrenched peach-tree-and-pickaninny mind-set that distinguished the true Old South.

Donkey

See **Mule.**

Drift fence

Such fences, common in the last third of the nineteenth century, were intended to stop the drift of cattle south in the winter, when instinct urged the critters to escape the cold and seek warmer weather elsewhere. They had nothing to do with snow-drifts. Snow fences belonged to a different era and were quite a different thing. Along some highways in the Panhandle and High Plains you can still see the remnants of snow fences, which were intended to allow snow to drift against the slats and thus prevent the roads from being entirely obscured. By the sixties snow fences had essentially disappeared.

Drift fences, incidentally, were a total failure. Though they succeeded in their goal—to stop cattle moving south in the winter and save cowboys the work of rounding them up—they had a deadly side effect: cattle instinctively moved south anyway, and in what were called the "big die-ups" of the 1880s whole herds piled up helplessly against the barbed wire and then froze to death, unable to ignore instinct and turn back. That was the end of the drift fence as well.

Driscoll, Clara

The much-touted Savior of the Alamo wasn't. That honor accurately belongs to Adina de Zavala, granddaughter of Lorenzo de Zavala, a signer of the Texas Declaration of Independence. Adina, who was also the moving force behind the preservation of the Spanish Governor's Palace in San Antonio, was the first to stir interest in identifying and saving the original mission grounds. Had Adina not preceded her, Clara Driscoll might well have directed her energies toward her neighborhood sewing circle.

In 1892 the State of Texas had already purchased the mission chapel from the Catholic Church. But unrecognized and in danger of being destroyed were the walls of the Alamo's long barracks or convent, where the major fighting occurred. Determined to prevent a tragedy, Miss Adina went to the wholesale grocery firm that owned the superstructure covering the near ruins and extracted from the owners a first option to buy the decrepit property, whose desirable location was the target of an Eastern hotel syndicate. Then she and her women's history group, which affiliated with the Daughters of the Republic of Texas in 1893, set about trying to raise funds to restore the convent and reestablish the courtyard.

Enter Clara Driscoll. Fresh from a tour of Europe, she lamented Texas' lack of impressive historical shrines, or so the story goes. Bored, she learned of the DRT's attempt to preserve the Alamo grounds and threw herself into the fray, using her wealthy father's name to dun the locals for cash. The total fell far short, though, and because of that Clara Driscoll earned her sobriquet. Since her family was rich, she simply asked Daddy for the money, thus buying the title "Savior of the Alamo."

So far the blue-blooded de Zavala and the silver-spooned Driscoll hadn't clashed. But *after* the DRT acquired the property, Clara horrified Adina by insisting that the group remove not only the newer eyesore—the decrepit structure that had been built over part of the barracks walls—but also the entire building, historical ruins and all. Adina insisted that preserving the walls was the whole point; Clara disagreed. The battle divided the DRT so bitterly that the feud ended up in state court, where Clara and her cash prevailed, assuming control of the DRT. Still, Adina had made her point; the society, despite the original opinion of its leader, decided not to raze the historical walls. And so they still stand today.

Drought

It can rain during a drought. Also correctly spelled and pronounced "drouth," a drought can be a total absence of rain or any prolonged dry spell with too little rain to sustain crops and livestock.

Drought is not confined to West Texas, either. For 35 of the last 100 years, some part of Texas, including East Texas, the Coastal Plains, and the Rio Grande Valley, has experienced drought.

Dr Pepper

Long a favorite in Texas, where it was invented in 1885, Dr Pepper is now the fifth-best-selling soft drink in America. The name, however, does not refer to the Waco pharmacist who first whipped it up. That was Charles Alderton, who started out serving it to regulars at Morrison's Old Corner Drug, where he worked. He named the soda-fountain concoction after a Dr. Pepper in Rural Retreat, Virginia. The pharmacist there had given Alderton's boss, Mr. Morrison, his very first job. According to folklore, the real Dr. Pepper had refused to let Morrison court his daughter. However, according to company spokesman Jim Ball, that story is fiction, as the girl in question was eight years old at the time. Rural Retreat has always billed itself as the home of the drink Dr Pepper, a claim that directly contradicts Waco's. Ball notes, though, that historical records for the Virginia pharmacy (which closed in 1994) contain no reference to sales of the beverage until the 1920s.

In 1988, Dr Pepper merged with the St. Louis-based 7-Up Company. The joint corporation thus formed became the third-largest soft drink company in the U.S. It maintains headquarters in Dallas.

Note: the "Dr" is never spelled out and is not followed by a period. At one time the period existed, but by about 1950 it had vanished from the company's logos and promotional art.

Drugstore cowboy

A term of derision for a pseudo-cowboy, but not a true cowboy's term. The real thing was more likely to call a novice dressed in Western clothes a mail-order cowboy or possibly a Rexall wrangler. There was also the term "goat-roper"—a real insult, and one that still exists today.

Dry county

Despite Texas' reputation as the buckle of the Bible Belt, 201 of its 254 counties are wet, allowing the public sale of liquor by the drink. The remaining 53 are dry, but that doesn't necessarily mean that you have to throw out your six-pack at a certain county line or that you can't get a bourbon and branch water if you wish. The sale of mixed drinks is prohibited by and large in dry counties, but residents may keep liquor in their homes (they have to buy it elsewhere, obviously) or buy it by the drink in private clubs. Though the concept of private clubs limits the consumption of liquor and keeps it indoors, the word private is misleading. Most restaurants and motels offer temporary membership to passers-through, so the thirsty traveler doesn't have to face a single boozeless night.

Wetness or dryness depends on local option; hence a dry county may contain wet precincts—Dallas County, for example—and a wet one may contain dry precincts—such as parts of the Heights in Houston.

Dryness of Texas

The image of Texas as a parched, sunbleached wasteland persists in the popular imagination, despite the fact that more of Texas is humid than dry. The state's three biggest cities, Houston, Dallas, and San Antonio, have average relative humidity percentages of 77, 65, and 67 respectively. Houston gets 45 inches of precipitation a year, more than Boston, Chicago, Washington, D.C., New York, or even Key West, Florida. Obviously, anyone who thinks Texas weather is all dry is all wet.

Dublin, Texas

The north central town of 2,700 wasn't named for the city in Ireland. The name comes from the nineteenth-century expression "double in," meaning "hurry up" or "come in on the double." The phrase was often used in pioneer towns to warn of imminent Indian raids.

Dust devil

Dust has nothing to do with the formation of these small whirlwinds, common across Texas but especially in its western half. The requirements are a hot day, a level surface, and a cool breeze that displaces the warmer air on the ground. If the wind picks up just as the two temperatures of air mingle, a spiraling, traveling dust devil is born. The miniature tornado inevitably picks up dirt and grit as it whips along, making itself easy to see. So much for the "dust." The "devil" is understandable if you or your car has ever gotten in one's way.

Eagle

Birders can find both the golden and bald eagles across most of Texas. The bald eagle, of course, is not really bald, as is the **buzzard.** From far away the eagle's white head feathers make it appear so. The golden eagle is golden only on its neck; the rest of its coloring is brown.

Eisenhower, Dwight David

As every schoolchild knows, Ike was one of two U.S. presidents born in Texas. (See **Johnson, Lyndon Baines.**) His birthplace was Denison, north of Dallas on the Oklahoma border. The Eisenhower family left Texas when Ike was just a baby, however, settling in Abilene, Kansas, where he grew up. Thus, despite his birthplace, he never considered himself a Texan but was always a Kansan first and foremost. Nonetheless, Texas proudly established two state parks in his name and considers him one of its own.

El Dorado

See **Cibola, Seven Cities of.**

Evans, Dale

A native of Uvalde, she was born Frances Octavia Smith on October 31, 1912. There is some confusion, however, over her exact real name. In 1954 she discovered, after requesting a copy of her birth certificate, that the document listed her as Lucille Wood Smith and, furthermore, stated that she had been born a day earlier than she supposed. At any rate, she adopted the name "Dale Evans" when she entered show business, and she is also known as Mrs. Roy Rogers. (Roy, by the way, started out life as Leonard Slye of Cincinnati.)

"Everything's big in Texas"

Patently untrue, this statement fails to take into consideration such petite but powerful Texans as **Ima Hogg** and **Clara Driscoll,** tiny hamlets such as Terlingua and Luckenbach, and miniature wallop-packers like the chile pequín and the silicon chip. See also **Tall Texan.**

"The Eyes of Texas"

The official song of the University of Texas at Austin, it is not—regardless of what many UT exes think—the state song, which is **"Texas, Our Texas."** Nonetheless, "The Eyes of Texas" is often performed at public functions across the state, where certainly UT alumni outnumber those from any other university in Texas.

"The Eyes of Texas" was not written intentionally as the UT song. It started out as a joke. UT's turn-of-the-century president was William Lambdin Prather, who frequently exhorted the student body to excel because, as he put it, "Ladies and gentlemen, the eyes of Texas are upon you." In 1903, a student named John Lang Sinclair, knowing that Prather was to attend a particular campus minstrel show, wrote "The Eyes of Texas" as a spoof, setting it to the tune of "I've Been Working on the Railroad." The song was an instant hit across campus, but it was not adopted officially as the UT song until Prather died two years later and students asked and received permission to sing it at his funeral.

Fajita

Not a Mexican food, fajitas do not come from the interior of Mexico and will not be found in any compendium of Mexican cooking, though the dishes called *arrecheras* and *tacos al carbón* are quite similar. Fajitas are truly Tex-Mex, combining Texas' beloved beef and barbecue-style cooking with flour tortillas, guacamole, and pico de gallo.

The invention of the fajita is lost in the mists of time. Because of its current popularity, lots of people claim credit for originating it long ago. Sonny Falcón, the former butcher and self-styled Fajita King who introduced it into the Austin area in the mid-sixties, says the fajita was a natural progression in the tradition of outdoor cooking that he enjoyed as a boy in the Rio Grande Valley in the thirties and forties. Valley inhabitants, through economic necessity as much as choice, used cheaper cuts of meat—beef ribs, *tripas*—for grilling, and Falcón contends that skirt steak, the cut of meat traditional for fajitas, was also a logical choice (he calls it "poor boy's filet"). Before the popularity of fajitas, butchers considered skirt steak a table trimming and not always a salable cut, and they often ground it for hamburger.

Honest-to-god fajitas are always made with skirt steak, not with round steak, sirloin, or any other substitute. As a result, a once cheap cut of meat has become rather pricey. Even worse is the substitution of chicken for the beef. Though the dish may be tasty, it is not a fajita. The name "fajita" implies beef, and the term "chicken fajita" is just as absurd as "vegetarian chili." A tony restaurant in Houston offered an even sillier version: lobster fajitas. And an Austin chef once produced rattlesnake fajitas.

Another requirement for real fajitas: the meat must be grilled (indoors or outdoors), not broiled or fried. Fajitas mandate flour tortillas; corn tortillas or any other bread won't do. Today most fajitas are marinated first—not an authentic step in the preparation—and then served with various combinations of guacamole, pico de gallo, sour cream, and cheese, garnishes that also are not authentic.

Because fajitas are traditionally made with skirt steak, many Texans think the word "fajita" means "little skirt." Actually, the Spanish word *faja* means "band" or "strap," referring to the shape of the elongated cut of the meat before it is grilled and sliced. The Spanish for "skirt" is *falda*.

See also **Burrito; Chili.**

Fannin, James W., Jr.

His name is always sounded on the roll call of Texas heroes, but it doesn't belong there. Colonel James Walker Fannin, Jr., was a man unfit for military leadership. Historians, and 150 intervening years, have been kind to him, but Colonel Fannin was not only inept but also foolish, as a look at the evidence will prove.

First of all, Fannin flatly refused aid to the Alamo. He commanded, at Goliad, the largest unit of Texas' ragtag army, and the assistance of his men might have meant victory for the Texans, but when messenger James Bonham rode in asking for help, Fannin gave him a solid no. On February 23, 1836, a week after Fannin's first refusal, Bonham again carried to him an urgent plea from Travis, alerting him that the Mexicans had arrived at the

Alamo. Though Fannin did set out eventually, he was clearly reluctant to go, and when one of his wagons broke down a short way from Goliad he welcomed the accident as a sign to turn back and forget about Travis and his men.

His decision to call off the trip led him to a fate no less horrible than that of the Alamo defenders. First he dispatched a hundred or so of his five hundred men to evacuate the population of Refugio and help the settlers flee the approaching Mexican Army. About a third of those men were caught and killed by the enemy; the rest scattered and fled. In the meantime, though Fannin had received unequivocal orders from General Sam Houston to retreat to Victoria, he delayed leaving, waiting instead for his Refugio contingent to report. When he learned too late that they had been defeated and captured by the Mexican Army, he and his men fled toward La Bahía fortress at Goliad, with Santa Anna's soldiers close behind.

Fannin had waited too long, and yet after a march of only a few miles he called a halt—in the middle of open prairie, with no usable cover and no available water, though woods and a creek were close by. Inevitably, the Mexicans caught up to him and surrounded his men. Fannin had two choices: surrender or slaughter. He chose surrender and, not being in a position to quibble about it, signed an unconditional surrender, leaving his men at the mercy of the victors.

Returned to Goliad and imprisoned there, Fannin's men were confident of being treated well, as prisoners of war deserved; one Mexican official even went so far as to reassure them they would soon be home again in the United States. But within a week the healthy prisoners were marched out of Goliad in three separate columns and shot in cold blood on the roadside. The wounded P.O.W.'s were executed outside the prison. About 27 men escaped the bloodbath, but some 350 died. Fannin was shot last, after being told of the fate of his men.

Colonel Fannin and his army have always been regarded by Texans as martyrs second only to those in the Alamo, but it was the Mexicans' vicious treatment of their captives that guaranteed that martyrdom. Certainly Fannin's behavior had little to do with it. Fury at the criminal treatment of his men led the attackers at

San Jacinto a month later to say not just **"Remember the Alamo!"** but "Remember the Alamo! Remember Goliad!"

Father of Texas

See **Austin, Stephen F.**

Fence-cutting wars

The clash between landowners who wanted their property kept strictly private and cattlemen who favored a wide-open range led, in 1883, to the brief but bloody fence-cutting wars, in which the anti-fence forces snipped their neighbors' offending barbed wire. But the fence-cutters weren't always the bad guys. As **barbed wire** grew more and more common on the range, ranchers fenced in their herds to improve stock (and farmers fenced them out to protect crops), but in the they process often cut off access to public water supplies and to grasslands on which smaller cowmen had depended. In Archer County, pro-wire cattlemen once fenced off all roads leading to the county seat. Hence the poorer and less powerful residents fought back, with wire cutters and at night. Their sneaky tactics didn't win them any friends, but the pro-wire faction behaved just as badly; as hostilities escalated, they often deliberately fenced off roads or rivers, just to cause hard feelings. The big cattlemen could see nothing but their own needs, while the smaller ones were unable to accept the end of the open range.

Despite their fame and intensity, the fence-cutting wars lasted only a year, 1883, when a drought had made Texas desperate for water and every creek and pond was coveted even more than usual. The next year the Texas Legislature made wire-cutting illegal, a law that still stands today, appearing in the criminal mischief section of the Texas Penal Code as a third-degree felony. Probably no other single historical event so deeply ingrained in Texans a fervor for the sanctity of private property.

Ferguson, Ma

Miriam Amanda Ferguson was Texas' first female governor, but—unlike the highly popular Ann Richards—she is no stellar role model for Texas' young women. Despite her election to Texas' highest office, she was a dutiful wife who ran for the job because her husband told her to.

James E. Ferguson had served as governor from 1915 to 1917, a term that ended ignominiously when he was impeached by the Legislature on ten charges, most them dealing with misapplication of public funds. He was thus ineligible to run again, so he persuaded his wife to take up the banner. She won twice, in 1924 and 1932, promising voters "two governors for the price of one." During her tenure, her husband kept an office next door to hers and attended official meetings in her place. Openly admitting "I don't know much about politics," Ma sought and followed his advice, often merely providing an official signature when it was needed. Thus her office as the U.S.'s second woman governor (after Nellie Tayloe Ross of Wyoming) was no great stride for womankind; if anything, it was a backslide.

Her nickname, "Ma," came not from her image as a dear gray-haired old mother—though she did have two daughters—but from the initials of her first two names. Her husband, despite beliefs to the contrary, was not called Pa. Texans always labelled him "Farmer Jim," after the typical member of his constituency.

Flag

See **Lone Star flag.**

Flag pledge

See **Lone Star flag.**

Flatness

It's a flat-out lie that Texas is flat. The elevation in the state ranges from sea level at the coast to 8,749 feet, the height of Guadalupe Peak in Culberson County. That means Texas' highest peak is much taller than the number-one mountain in 37 other states, including North and South Dakota, Kentucky, Virginia, and West Virginia—none of which is exactly considered flat.

Flour tortilla

See **Burrito; Fajita.**

Flower, state

See **Bluebonnet.**

"Foat Wuth"

Though it is certainly an acceptable pronunciation of that city's name, it is by no means the only one. Many people who are as native to Texas as those with a heavier drawl pronounce the name just as it is spelled. Anyone, however, might be apt to drop the r's for show on a trip up East.

Four Sixes (6666)

The famous 6666 Ranch, established by Samuel Burk Burnett in 1867, was not won in a poker hand that featured four sixes. Burnett picked the name and the brand because he had once held a poker hand with that particular four of a kind. With typical Texas accuracy, local legend soon contended that the ranch was part of his gambling winnings, but the story is a myth.

Burnett's brother flipped Burk's brand and used 9999 for his own, but no poker story embellished the acquisition of his property.

Frito

A Texan food, despite its Hispanic name. The corn chip was created in San Antonio by a Mexican who hawked his son-of-tostada fried snack in various local cafés. In 1932 a certain Elmer Doolin paid the anonymous Frito inventor $100 for his recipe and list of customers because the original vendor wanted to return home to Mexico. Doolin fiddled with the ingredients and the shape and christened his chip the Frito, a Spanish word meaning fried. Today Doolin's company is the giant snack-food corporation Frito-Lay, headquartered in Dallas.

The identity of the original Frito creator is unknown. One story, though unsubstantiated, has it that a certain Don Gustavo Olguín of Oaxaca, who died in 1981, was the real Mr. Frito. In Spanish slang the word frito can also mean "annoyed," and that is certainly how Don Gustavo must have felt when he contemplated the success of Elmer Doolin.

Garner, John Nance

See **Bluebonnet.**

Garrett, Pat

While the sheriff of Lincoln County, New Mexico, he made a name for himself by shooting **Billy the Kid** dead. But the feat was no fancy showdown or display of bravado. Garrett surprised Billy in the dark, in a bedroom of the ranch where he was hiding out, and shot him twice in the chest. After ridding the West of such a famous criminal, Garrett became famous himself, but because of Billy's youth and popularity his action was as much condemned as approved. (For instance, he did not win a second term as sheriff.)

Although Garrett, by virtue of his office, automatically became Billy's enemy, they had once been friends and fellow gamblers. But that friendship didn't stop Garrett from a ruthless pursuit of the young murderer. He captured Billy, who was want-ed for, among other things, the murder of a local rancher, and threw him and his sidekicks in jail. He reveled in the congratulations for a while—until Billy escaped, killing two guards. Garrett took Billy's actions personally; no doubt he thought a dead Billy the Kid would be better than another embarrassing escape. Hence the ambush in the dark.

Garrett claimed immunity to the charm of Billy's romantic (and much exaggerated) exploits, but couldn't resist writing his own *Authentic Life of Billy the Kid*, which was as thrilling—and as wholly inaccurate—as any other dime novel.

Like many Texas lawmen, Garrett lived and died by the gun, killed by a neighbor after a drawn-out feud over pastureland. By most accounts the neighbor acted in self-defense, but some versions say Garrett was surprised and murdered in cold blood, just as he himself had dispatched his most famous quarry.

Gas

The word may mean either gasoline or natural gas. Both are hydrocarbons. Gasoline is a liquid, natural gas a true gas. Gasoline, an automotive fuel, is a volatile, flammable liquid hydrocarbon refined from crude oil. Natural gas, best known for its use in cooking and heating, is a highly compressible mixture of hydrocarbons that occurs naturally in a gaseous form. Natural gas is called sour gas if it contains hydrogen sulfide and sweet gas if it does not.

When you smell a gas leak, you are smelling not the natural gas itself but harmless chemicals such as Mercaptan. Because natural gas is odorless, the stinky Mercaptan is added to it to alert you to a leak. A leak is dangerous not because natural gas is poisonous—it isn't—but because of the risk of explosion, if both oxygen and a source of ignition are present, or the possibility of poisoning by carbon monoxide, a by-product of combustion that may accumulate if there is insufficient ventilation.

What we call natural gas is but one of the gases produced along with other fossil fuels in certain sediments. The other gases are no less natural but far less useful to humankind.

Gila monster

Like **saguaro** cactus, the Gila monster is a frequent element of Texas desert scenes, but a fallacious one. Gila monsters do not live in Texas but only in deserts farther west.

Gimme cap

The Texas version of a baseball cap, it features an adjustable band at the back and a logo or slogan across the front. Originally most gimme caps touted oil-related products, farm machinery, or other similarly Texan industries and were favored by rednecks and bluecollar workers. Now the headgear has become so popular that even ad agencies, magazines, and art museums—Texan or not—offer them to the public.

The name "gimme cap" derived from the practice of giving away the hats for promotional purposes or providing them to employees as a source of free advertising; supposedly the term is a shortened form of "Gimme one of them caps." However, few gimme caps today are free.

Globe Theatre

The famous London theater, where most of Shakespeare's plays debuted, was built in 1598, burned in 1613, was promptly rebuilt, and then was destroyed for good by the Puritans in 1644. However, the Globe exists today—in Odessa, which boasts a detailed and accurate replica of the theater. The Odessa Globe stages Shakespearean plays every year, alternated with more typical West Texas fare such as the "Brand New Opree."

Goddess of Liberty

The draped figure atop the **State Capitol** carries not a torch, like the Statue of Liberty's, but a five-pointed star covered in 23-karat gold leaf. She has been called Pallas Athena, after the Greek goddess of wisdom, and also the Goddess of Justice, but she was modeled after no one in particular. The 3000-pound statue is not the original, which was removed in 1986 and replaced with an exact copy cast in aluminum instead of zinc alloy.

Supposedly the goddess faces south, toward the Colorado River, because at the time the Capitol was built, in 1881, anti-Union feelings still ran high. True enough, but the Capitol sits on a gentle rise just north of the river, so the statue, and the building's face, naturally follow the view.

Goliad Massacre

A mere two weeks after the fall of the **Alamo** came Texas' second-worst tragedy ever: the Mexican army's slaughter of almost 400 captured Texas troops serving under Colonel **James W. Fannin, Jr.** Because Fannin surrendered to General José Urrea, his men were confident of receiving decent treatment at the hands of their captors, under the traditional tenets of international law. The Mexicans, however, acting on the orders of Santa Anna, shot the Texans, including the wounded. Some 27 escaped. The Mexicans unquestionably acted shamefully, although after the event documents proved that Fannin had signed an unconditional surrender, essentially giving them the right to dispose of the prisoners as they saw fit. Possibly the Mexicans would have killed the Texans anyway, but when he signed the unconditional surrender Fannin surely knew what might be in store. Texas considered the event an outrage and a massacre; Mexico termed it an incident and an execution. Compare the **Black Bean Episode.**

Gone to Texas

A catchphrase of the early nineteenth century, it originally meant merely that a man or a family had headed southwest to settle in the new territory of Texas, which even early on was considered a wild and woolly land. But because so many wanted men fled to the isolated territory to escape the law up East, the phrase came to be a euphemism for "on the lam." (Whether Texas' unsavory reputation or the arrival of the riffraff came first is hard to say.) "Gone to Texas" was often abbreviated "GTT."

Gran Quivira

See **Cibola, Seven Cities of.**

Grapefruit

Texas' biggest citrus crop, grapefruit got its name not because it resembles grapes in taste or looks but because it grows on trees in thick, grapelike clusters.

Greer County

See **Boundaries of Texas.**

Gun

See **Gunfight; Colt .45.**

Gunfight

A fact of life during the Old West, gunfights nevertheless are nearly always portrayed inaccurately in movies. Most gunfights were not showdowns or shoot-outs in the streets, with anxious and excited townfolk looking on as two hard-faced men slowly marched toward each other until one drew, both shot, and one fell dead. Much romanticized by Hollywood, gunfights were more likely to occur in the heat of anger in a saloon, perhaps after a dispute over politics or cards, and usually at point-blank range. Showdowns were extremely rare; ambushes or sneak attacks were more common, improving as they did the odds of survival for the offensive side. When gunfighters (or gunfighters and lawmen) did arrange what was essentially the Western equivalent of a duel, they usually stood quite close together—not the 30 or more feet portrayed in movies—which is why death, and not mere injury, was a certainty.

Another element of the gunfight usually missing from a contemporary reenactment is the smoke. For most of the duration of the wild West, revolvers required black powder cartridges, which produced huge clouds of black smoke (and a terrific stink).

Despite their popularity in motion pictures, real gunfights were quite rare. Death by violence was not the norm in the Old West. Being thrown from or kicked by a horse was much more likely to be the cause of a cowboy's sudden demise.

Two more corrections of gunfight misinformation: Most men wore their holsters high on the hip. The low-slung holster might look sexier to a modern eye, but it was less comfortable and made it more difficult to "clear leather." Also, fanning a gun—depressing the trigger and using the palm of the opposite hand to repeatedly hit the hammer—was uncommon and often unreliable, though the practice lends a certain panache to stars of the silver screen.

See also **Colt .45; Quick-draw artist.**

Gypped

According to most dictionaries, the word is derived from "gypsies," the itinerant people who were always suspected of cheating or duping their customers and benefactors. But Western lexicographer Ramon Adams suggested that the cowboy used "gypped" or "gyppy" to describe water containing gypsum, which gave it a bitter taste and rendered it undrinkable, leaving the poor cowboy understandably feeling cheated.

Hackamore

A wonderfully Anglicized version of the Spanish word *jáquima*, a type of horse bridle. Borrowed from the Mexican vaquero and mangled by the Texas cowboy.

Hardin, John Wesley

He started his killing streak in 1868 at the tender age of 14, when he murdered an ex-slave who had bested him in a fistfight. From then on the native of Bonham, Texas, was continually on the run from justice. He added a few victims a year to his total—shooting most of them multiple times, and usually without provocation—until by age 21 he had killed 39 men.

Ironically, though Hardin was without a doubt guilty of many cold-blooded killings, the shooting he was finally tried for was a clear case of self-defense. In a saloon in Comanche County, Hardin had been accosted by a man he didn't know. Unperturbed, Hardin offered the man a drink and turned to order it from the bartender. An onlooker shouted, and Hardin turned back to see the fellow reaching for his gun. Hardin fired first and asked questions later, learning that the dead man was the sheriff of nearby Brown County, who had wanted Hardin not on any particular charge but because he thought Texas would be well rid of the gunman. Hardin fled and was free for two more years before the Texas Rangers tracked him down in Florida. His story of self-defense, supported by witnesses, earned him a 25-year sentence instead of a hanging.

Pardoned in 1894, Hardin established a law practice in El Paso, having studied the discipline while in prison. (Hence he gave a distinct meaning to the phrase "criminal lawyer.") He still was unable to avoid minor brushes with the law though, occasionally at the hands of two local constables, the father-and-son Selmans. Irate because the younger Selman had harassed his latest girl-friend, whose virtue was none too pristine, Hardin insulted the constable, who shortly thereafter walked up behind him in the Acme Saloon and shot him in the back of the head. It was clearly murder, and yet Selman got away with it, stating that Hardin easily could have spotted him in the mirror over the bar. But justice prevailed; less than a year later Selman himself was shot to death in an alley by a deputy marshal named George Scarborough.

See also **Gunfight.**

Haynes, Racehorse

His real first name is not Racehorse, of course. It is Richard. The nickname refers not to fast talking or quick thinking in the courtroom, however, though both those abilities apply. The flamboyant Houston lawyer acquired it during a football game in high school when, carrying the ball, he attempted to outrun his pursuers by heading sideways across the field. "That kid must think he's a racehorse," said his coach.

Hereford

The cattle aren't named after the town; the town is named for the cattle, a white-faced, red-backed breed that populates the surrounding Panhandle grazelands. However, the famous whitefaces were first developed not in Texas but in Herefordshire, England (the county seat of which is Hereford as well).

To a cowboy, a Hereford also meant a dress suit, because of its white shirtfront.

Hill, Dr. John

Many Texans assume he was a killer, but he was never found guilty of murder. He was the husband of Houston equestrian and socialite Joan Robinson Hill, who in March of 1969 died of a mysterious and massive infection. Joan, a theretofore healthy woman of 38, had suffered horrible diarrhea and vomiting for days while her husband, a physician, treated her at home. When she was finally admitted to a hospital, doctors could find no cause for her severe illness, and she died within 24 hours.

John Hill was suspected of having caused her death by somehow introducing into her system a deadly bacterium, possibly by means of a particular French pastry he had carefully given to her and watched her eat. Indicted by a grand jury, he was charged with murder by omission, that is, failure to provide proper medical care. **Racehorse Haynes** represented him, and the resulting case—full of accusation, innuendo, and medicalese—eventually ended in a mistrial.

Three years later, John Hill was shot and killed by a masked intruder who had lain in wait in his home. Again, River Oaks society had another scandal on its hands: Had Ash Robinson, the elderly and devoted father of Joan Robinson Hill, arranged the doctor's murder? No concrete evidence linked him to Hill's death, though three other people were arrested in the case. The confessed killer, while out on bond, was later killed by a policeman in a bar, and two women accomplices were convicted and sent to prison.

Hilton, Conrad

See **Hilton Hotels.**

Hilton Hotels

The first hotel of the famous chain owned by entrepreneur Conrad Hilton was built in Dallas in 1925. However, Hilton managed his very first hotel, the Mobley, in 1919 in little Cisco, Texas, a town so proud of that debut that it later rechristened its main street Conrad Hilton Avenue. (His first dozen or so hotels were all in small Texas towns). But by his own admission, the hotel nearest and dearest to Hilton's heart was the El Paso Hilton, which many Texans erroneously consider the first Hilton. The luxurious edifice was built in 1930 despite the shattered stock market that threatened its completion. Hilton's mother—a notoriously poor tipper—lived at the El Paso Hilton for years, and Conrad once maintained his headquarters there.

Hogg, Ima

The wealthy Houston philanthropist, who died in 1975 at age 93, was not named as a joke. Ima was her real name. Her father, James Stephen Hogg, Texas' first native-born governor, named her after the romantic heroine of a long epic poem written by his brother, who died before she was born. One has to marvel at his apparent ignorance of the combination of names. It was so amusing that there soon arose the popular legend of her sisters, Ura and Wera, who allegedly died young. Actually, Miss Ima had only brothers, three of them, all with unremarkable names.

If Miss Ima's name was unforgettable, so were her gifts to the people of Texas. She restored the Brazoria County plantation where her father had grown up and donated it to the state as a park. She bought the land and buildings of historic Winedale and gave them to the University of Texas. She also left Bayou Bend, her fifteen-acre River Oaks home, and its invaluable antique Texas furnishings to the Houston Museum of Fine Art.

Homestead Law

Texas, from its inception a fervent protector of its citizens' property rights, demonstrates its intent nowhere more strongly than in its homestead law. While Texas was still a republic its congress made illegal the seizing of a debtor's home, leading to the widely held belief that in Texas you cannot lose your house, no matter what. Actually, you can. First of all, the protected house must be your homestead, not a vacation cabin, for example, or a second residence. Second of all, you can lose it anyway. Most creditors have no claim, it's true, but a homeowner who defaults can lose his property to the holders of the purchase mortgage or to anyone who improved the property but was not paid (say, the guy who built your deck). If encumbrances on the property—that is, claims against it—existed before you declared the real estate your homestead, you could be in trouble. And of course, if you don't pay your taxes as Uncle Sam says you should, the IRS can take it away.

"Hook 'em!"

The solidarity cry of the **University of Texas** at Austin relates to its mascot, the Longhorn; the hook 'em sign, the index and little fingers raised with the thumb and middle fingers curled down, symbolizes the mascot's horns and, UT fans hope, its goring power. However, the phrase "Hook 'em" was first used in ranch life, when, during branding, cowboys would call it out to tease or encourage an imprisoned cow undergoing the ignominy of branding.

The creation of the hook 'em sign itself is credited to Harley Clark, Jr., UT's head cheerleader in 1955 and now a state district judge in Austin.

Hoosegow

Another colorful cowboyism, this one is the muddled Texas version of *juzgado*, the Spanish word for "tribunal" or "courtroom." Used nationwide, it is slang for "jail."

Hoover hog

See **Armadillo.**

Horny toad

Despite its popular name, the horny toad is not a toad. It's a lizard—a horned lizard, if you want to be precise. Few natives call it anything but a horny toad, except students and alumni of Texas Christian University, who term their mascot the horned frog. But both "toad" and "frog" are wrong. *Phrynosoma cornutum*, the

Texas horned lizard, is a reptile, not an amphibian. In fact, it is a descendant of the dinosaur.

So much for the "toad" half of the name. Now, let's consider the "horny." Horny toads aren't. Usually they mate but once a year, in the spring. Although males are equipped with not one but two sexual organs, called hemipenes, the "horny" refers to the critter's spikes and horns that provide protection as well as charm.

Some people believe that horny toads have the ability to squirt blood from their eyes. The idea is laughable, but it is also true. So few people have witnessed the phenomenon that most scoff at the very suggestion. When a horny toad is frightened or angry, its blood pressure rises so rapidly in reaction that its head swells up with blood and a thin stream breaks out of pores in the corners of its eyelids. Whether deliberate anger or involuntary fear causes the blood-squirting is uncertain, but it is no fable. The Texas horned lizard, however, is the only species capable of this feat. The state's other two horned lizards, the round-tailed and mountain short-horned, do not squirt blood.

The horny toad is not extinct, or even endangered, although its tourist-trap popularity in the fifties reduced its numbers so considerably that the state began protecting it in 1967. Like most longtime Texans, horny toads prefer the country to the city, which chemicals and construction have made an unfit home. But though it is not as public a figure as it once was, Texas' own little triceratops is still around.

See also **Old Rip.**

Horseback riding

Despite what some Yankees might think, not everyone in Texas can ride a horse, and those that do aren't necessarily cowboys and cowgirls. Since 1940 Texas has grown steadily more urbanized, and its citizenry who do know how to mount and control a horse are just as likely to have learned on an English saddle at a riding academy as on a workhorse for a farm or ranch.

Hot sauce

Texas' favorite condiment is hot because of the jalapeños it contains, not because of its temperature. But by now even Yankees know that. Texans borrowed the idea of hot sauce from Mexico, where various *salsas* accompany every meal. Real hot sauce contains no sugar or other unacceptable ingredients, and it could never be confused with ketchup. It is a fiery mixture of jalapeños, onions, tomatoes, vinegar, salt, and spices. The granddaddy of Texas hot sauce is Pace picante sauce, which has been produced in San Antonio since 1947. To Texas' shock, Pace reached an agreement in 1994 with Campbell Soup Company of New Jersey to become a subsidiary of the food giant. However, Pace officials reassured their alarmed customers that the hot sauce would continue to be prepared in San Antonio by veteran *salseros*.

See also **Pico de gallo.**

Houston, Sam

Texas' greatest statesman, he was at various times the commander in chief of the Texas Army, the president of the Republic, the U.S. senator from the State of Texas, and finally governor. But despite his stellar military and political careers, Sam Houston had his troubles and his faults.

In 1929, Marquis James's Pulitzer prize-winning biography *The Raven* took its title from the Indian nickname Houston acquired during his boyhood, when he befriended and occasionally lived with the Cherokee in Tennessee. His parents were Caucasian but—in a great honor for a white—he was adopted as a son by Chief John Jolly, who first christened him the Raven. That was not his only Indian name, however; during his trading days among the Arkansas Cherokee in the early 1830s, he was generally known as Big Drunk.

Besides a fondness for the bottle (which, incidentally, would have been enough reason for Stephen F. Austin to turn him down as a colonist), Houston, like many Texas heroes, always had problems with his domestic life. After a spectacular ascent in Tennessee politics—he went from the study of law to the office of governor in nine years—he took his first wife, sixteen-year-old

Eliza Allen, in 1829. Within three and a half months she left him, returning to her parents' home. Amid the ensuing scandal and speculation, Houston resigned after only two years in office. That was how he ended up in Arkansas, living and trading with the Cherokee. Ever the gentleman, Houston never revealed the reason why his bride fled, and as a result his contemporaries reviled him for what they imagined was horrendous treatment of the girl. Later historians theorized that the teenage Eliza was simply not ready for marriage, especially marriage to a prominent statesman, or that she still favored her former fiancé. Their union was not dissolved, however, until years later when Houston was president of the Republic of Texas and was able to issue his own divorce decree.

At any rate, while in Arkansas Houston lived with a squaw, Tiana Rogers (also called Tiana, or Diana, Gentry), who is usually referred to as his wife even though at the time he was still tied to Eliza. Neither Indians nor frontiersmen were particular about that kind of thing, especially since the woman involved was an older widow. Houston left Tiana to go to Texas, and in his absence she died. Romantics regard Tiana as the great love of Houston's life and claim her influence inspired Houston's lifelong benevolence toward Indians. Actually his attitude stemmed from his youthful friendship with the Cherokee.

Ten years later, after his impressive performance at San Jacinto had led to an inevitable but uneventful election as president of the Republic, Houston married officially for the second time, and finally it took. Margaret Moffette Lea, 26 years his junior, bore him eight children, made him cut down on his drinking, and even persuaded him to join the Baptist church.

Though Sam Houston is considered the prototype of all Texans—tough, tall, brave—his leadership of Texas wasn't all that glorious. He lobbied hard for statehood, rather than reveling in Texas' status as an independent nation, and instead of taking a hard line with Mexico and the Indian nations, he tried to placate them all. For his reserve he is variously excoriated or praised. In contrast, his successor, Mirabeau B. Lamar, who was his physical and temperamental opposite—slender, shy, visionary—advocated keeping Texas a free state and waging war on both the Indian and border frontiers.

In 1859, with his presidency and senatorship behind him, Houston ran for governor. Victorious, he tackled the issue of the day: secession. But he was not in favor of it. He opposed it, denouncing its proponents and lobbying for a compromise. He refused to recognize Texas' Secession Convention of 1861, denied Texas' ties to the Confederacy, and urged the U.S. Army in Texas to resist the rebels. Furious at this display of disloyalty, the secessionists forced him out of office. When he died in 1863, he received no accolades or eulogies; Texas had turned its back on the hero of San Jacinto.

See also **"Remember the Alamo!"**

Hughes, Howard

Born in Houston on Christmas Eve, 1905, the rich and eccentric Howard Hughes was actually Howard Robard Hughes, Jr. His wealth came from his father, Howard Robard Hughes, Sr., whose invention of the **Hughes drill bit** revolutionized the oil industry. Thus the younger Howard inherited his original fortune—which was considerably less than one million dollars, even including patent rights to the Hughes bit. He was a brilliant businessman, however, and by the time of his death half a century later he had turned the legacy into a staggering billion dollars or more. His wealth was so great only estimates are possible.

While still a teenager, Howard Hughes took over the management of his father's corporation, Hughes Tool Company, and reorganized it to his satisfaction. He also bought up what stock he did not own. Then, having taken care of home business, he turned his attention to movies, women, and planes. He moved to California and soon made his name in Hollywood with three acclaimed films, *Hell's Angels* (1930), *The Front Page* (1931), and *Scarface* (1932). He launched the careers of Jean Harlow and Jane Russell and romanced other beauties such as Billie Dove, Ava Gardner, and Katharine Hepburn. Later in the thirties he set air speed records for transcontinental and round-the-world flights. In the early forties he designed the largest aircraft ever flown, the *Spruce Goose*, a huge seaplane made entirely of wood to save metal during wartime. It was flown exactly once, by Hughes himself. Hughes, by the way, detested the name *Spruce Goose*. He always referred to it as the HX-19.

Flying was the indirect cause of Hughes' renowned eccentricity. In 1946, he had a third plane crash, in which he was severely injured. Though he recovered, Hughes gradually began withdrawing from society, renouncing his former image as dashing playboy and daring aviator. He saw only a few trusted employees and directed his companies, which included RKO Pictures and TWA, from afar. By 1966 he was a complete recluse. He moved into a Las Vegas penthouse at the Desert Inn Hotel and Casino, which he owned, and though he traveled widely up until his death, he never again appeared in public. (He broke silence only once, in 1972, declaring in a news conference over long distance telephone from the Bahamas that a biography written by Clifford Irving was a fake and that he had never authorized the book.) Because of his secretive life, stories of his eccentricity abounded: He ate only a few odd foods; he received visitors while in bed; he was terribly afraid of germs and cigarette smoke; he had immersed himself in a strange religious cult; he refused to cut his hair or nails.

Hughes died on April 5, 1976, en route to Houston's Methodist Hospital on a chartered jet from Acapulco, where he had been staying. His wasted body weighed only about ninety pounds, but neither his hair nor his nails were absurdly long. He was a frequent user of codeine, and though rumor had it that the actual cause of his death was an overdose—deliberate or not, self-inflicted or not—doctors proclaimed the reason was actually kidney failure.

Within weeks of his death, the first of more than 40 alleged Hughes wills began appearing across the country. The most famous was the so-called Mormon will, in which a Utah gas station attendant named Melvin Dummar, among others, stood to benefit to the tune of $100 million. Dummar said he had once come across a dirty, bedraggled old man in the Utah desert, given him a lift, and lent him a quarter. The old man, so the story went, was Howard Hughes. Dummar became an instant celebrity, but in 1978 a Nevada district court dismissed the Mormon will as fake.

Down the drain, along with Dummar's hopes, went those of Rice University and University of Texas, each of which had been left one thirty-second of the estate, about $50 million. Hughes attended Rice University for less than a year between 1923 and 1924. He never went to UT.

A second major question, in the wake of Hughes' death, was that of his state of residence. Both Texas and California stood to collect hefty sums in inheritance tax from the Hughes estate. The two states began a five-year legal wrangle over the issue—including three appearances before the U.S. Supreme Court—while his relatives insisted that he was a resident of Nevada, which has no inheritance tax. Though Hughes was a native Texan, he had left the state shortly after his father's death and had not resided there full-time since. Still, he had frequently listed a Houston house address on tax returns, and he was heading there at the time of his death. Not surprisingly, a Houston probate court ruled he was a Texan. Eventually California and Texas compromised, and in 1984 Texas received the first of two payments of about $25 million.

In the meantime, a Houston judge had determined that Hughes left no valid will. Not all the alleged Hughes wills were forgeries, by any means; some were clearly written by the billionaire himself. But in those cases the documents lacked appropriate signatures, notarization, or what-have-you, rendering them legally worthless. Thus, because he died intestate, Hughes's huge fortune went to his family—and, of course, to their lawyers—though it was obvious that he had never intended for family or government to acquire any of his wealth. His purpose, as indicated in the invalid wills he left, was to leave his money to charities and for medical research.

Because Hughes had no children from either of his two marriages—to Ella Rice in 1925 and Jean Peters in 1957—his fortune was divided chiefly among 22 cousins. Another beneficiary was actress Terry Moore, who said she had been Hughes' third wife and won a settlement on the basis of her claim.

Hughes drill bit

The creator of the bit that revolutionized the oil and gas industry was not the curious and filthy-rich **Howard Hughes** of movie-production and aviation fame but his father, Howard Robard Hughes, Sr. The more famous Hughes originally acquired his wealth from his father's design and creation of a patented drill bit that is correctly called the Hughes Rock Bit. It was not the first drill bit, by any means, but the first *rotary* drill bit, whose revolving, steel-toothed cutting surfaces ground and crushed rock rather than beating against it. In many cases Hughes' bit was able to drill through rock that had otherwise proved impenetrable. The invention allowed oil and gas exploration to spread to formations that were previously considered untouchable, opening up millions of acres of land.

Humble, Texas

Though the town of Humble, in Harris County, is an oil town, it was not named for Humble Oil and Refining Company (now Exxon) but for P. S. Humble, its founder.

Hurricane

Another Spanish word borrowed and Anglicized. The original was *huracán*. Although U.S. weather services have, since 1979, used male as well as female names for the vicious storms, Texas' best-known hurricanes have all had women's names, such as Carla (1961, the largest hurricane ever in Texas) and Beulah (1967, which spawned the most tornadoes, 115). Texas' worst hurricane ever was nameless, occurring years before the practice of naming the storms began in 1953. It was the Great Storm of 1900, which savaged Galveston that September, destroying the city and killing at least 6,000 and maybe as many as 8,000 people. Galveston never fully recovered.

See also **Cyclone; Tornado; Weather.**

"If I owned hell and Texas . . ."

The famous quote about Texas was undoubtedly made by a non-Texan. In full the line is "If I owned hell and Texas, I'd rent out Texas and live in hell." It is usually attributed to Philip Sheridan, a Union soldier who served in Texas both before and after the Civil War and who eventually attained the rank of general. However, the quote never appears in his memoirs, nor does any other negative comment about Texas.

Immigrant

Texas is a land of immigrants. Starting in the seventeenth century, Spaniards, Mexicans, and Anglos in succession trickled and then poured into Texas, overcoming its isolation to pursue its opportunities. But one large group of early immigrants is rarely mentioned: Indians, who were often displaced from their homelands farther east by white men eager to exploit the country's rich natural resources for themselves.

In 1818, accepting an offer of resettlement from the white man's government, the Cherokee left their ancestral homes in the southeastern United States and moved in along the Trinity and Sabine rivers near Nacogdoches. They were followed by groups of Delaware, Shawnee, Chickasaw, Choctaw, and Kickapoo as well as much smaller tribes, mostly agricultural peoples anxious to resume their traditional lifestyles and escape the white man's curious and hostile world. Unfortunately, the Mexican government proved just as troublesome as the American one. The Indians encountered endless difficulties trying to gain title to their land and often faced the hostility of a new but similar group of whites. Eventually most of the Indians left—unlike the rest of Texas' immigrants. See **Indians.**

Indian blanket

The brilliant red wildflower, whose petals are tipped with vivid yellow, earned its name not just because Indians prized those colors in blankets and other goods but also because the flower blankets Texas, appearing practically statewide and blooming most profusely from April to June. The asterlike flower is sometimes confused with **Indian paintbrush.**

Indian paintbrush

A bright red-orange wildflower, it often mingles in the spring with bluebonnets. It is similar in color to the Indian blanket, but occurs less widely and appears a little earlier, from March to May. The color is produced not by the flowers, by the way, but by the surrounding floral leaves, called bracts. The flowers themselves are an unimpressive cream color.

Indians

Because of its size and wilderness, Texas in the nineteenth century was the home of at least 40 distinct Indian tribes, from horse-mad, war-happy Plains bands to peace-loving, often Christian tillers of the soil. Many were indigenous to Texas, but many were not—for instance, the best-known of all, the Comanche. Texas' native peoples included, in its western regions, the Lipan, Mescalero, and Jumano subunits of the Apache and, in East Texas, the highly civilized Caddo. There are scores more, most with names unfathomable to English speakers: Orocoquiza, Pampopa, Xarame. But just as many Indians in Texas were braves-come-lately. Branches of the Cherokee, Shawnee, Delaware, and Kickapoo packed up and moved to Texas from the Southeast in the early 1800s as the white men steadily moved westward, pushing them from their longtime homes. (See **Immigrant.**) Fierce hunters such as the Comanche and Kiowa were forced southward into Texas by the even fiercer Sioux. Many coastal tribes were also indigenous to Texas and even more deadly, like the Karankawa and Tonkawa, who, whether or not they were actually cannibalistic, managed to terrorize early explorers thoroughly.

All of those Indians called Texas home, but it is the evocative names and hair-raising anecdotes of the Plains tribes that pepper the first third of Texas' history—Iron Jacket, Adobe Walls, the Parker's Fort raid, the Salt Creek massacre, **Cynthia Ann Parker** and her halfbreed son, **Quanah Parker.** Their famous and powerful cultures are now gone, their domains long fallen to the white man. Now only two tribes still live in the Lone Star state, and they were, and still are, minor in terms of population and Texas history.

The combined Alabama-Coushatta tribe is a fairly recent arrival, having moved to Texas in 1807 and settled along the Trinity River. Former Indian trader Sam Houston, a champion of all Indians, was instrumental in getting the state to deed 1,280 acres to the Alabama-Coushatta, giving them a permanent home. The Tiguas, who settled in Ysleta, near El Paso, three centuries ago, are a Catholic tribe that is the oldest identifiable ethnic group in the state. Their tribal property covers only 97 acres.

So what happened to the Comanche, the Apache, and the other Indian nations? Many of them, like the Tonkawa, simply died out, being so few in number that they were unable to resist the encroachment of the white man, complete with his gun that spoke six times, his deceit, and his disease. In a way, the fate of the better-known Plains tribes was even worse, and it resulted from an early conflict in Texas and U.S. relations.

When Texas joined the Union in 1845, its terms of annexation strictly stated that all land within Texas' arbitrarily set boundaries would continue to belong to Texas, not to the U.S. However, under federal policy the U.S. was responsible for the Indians, or, as most contemporaries referred to the matter, the "Indian problem." Hence, when Texas became a state, many tribes found that they were automatically stripped of their land and suddenly under the jurisdiction of, as Anglo negotiators liked to put it, the Great White Father. Thus feelings of bad blood, always present between white and red, grew worse. Many peaceable agricultural tribes readily agreed to relocation, but the Plains tribes, who considered the Texas Panhandle and surrounding buffalo-rich land theirs alone, rejected the idea out of hand.

During the Civil War the isolated pioneers on Texas' western and northwestern frontiers suffered endlessly at the hands of the red raiders who, justifiably incensed at the whites' invasion of their hunting grounds, slaughtered and scalped the intruders and looted and burned their cabins and forts. During Reconstruction, though, the federal government was once again able to address the issue of Indian depredations. At major peace talks at Medicine Lodge, Kansas, in 1867, the federal government offered to resettle the troublemaking tribes in Indian Territory (Oklahoma). Again, some tribes agreed, but the Comanche, Kiowa, and a few others okayed the idea—in theory. They considered the United States and Texas two separate entities, as indeed they had once been. They promised not to wage war on the U.S., but to their way of thinking Texas was a different place.

They accepted the land the government assigned them, in the middle of the buffalo grounds, but delayed moving their families and undertook more raids and attacks. In retaliation, buffalo hunters and other white men blatantly trespassed on Indian property, while the Great White Father carefully looked the other way. Naturally, the Comanche, particularly the Quahadi, and allied tribes redoubled their efforts to oust the invaders, and brought down upon themselves the wrath of the U.S. Army. In a series of furious campaigns the soldiers steadily closed in upon the "red vermin," using the same unrelenting tactics they had so deplored in the Indians' hands. In one instance Colonel Ranald

Mackenzie trapped a whole village in the Palo Duro Canyon. He spared the Indians but struck what was in a way a far crueler blow by killing 1,400 of their horses, leaving the tribes completely vulnerable. By 1874 most of the Plains tribes had surrendered, and even the superproud Quahadi band gave it up and headed sorrowfully for Fort Sill, Oklahoma, the headquarters of the Indian reservation. Today Texas has a history indelibly colored by its mistreated, misunderstood Indians and an environment almost totally barren of their troubled and fascinating influence.

Iraan, Texas

The town has nothing to do with Iran, no matter how similar it might appear. Iraan is pronounced "Ira Ann" and in fact comes from those two Christian names, which belonged to a couple named Yates on whose ranch oil was discovered in the late twenties.

Inspired by the stark and primitive scenery surrounding Iraan, oil worker V. T. Hamlin, who lived there during the boom, created the comic-strip caveman Alley Oop.

Ireland, Texas

The tiny burg in Coryell County wasn't founded by lads from the old country. The town is named for John Ireland, a two-term governor of Texas in the 1880s.

Ivory-billed woodpecker

See **Woodpecker, ivory-billed.**

Jackalope

The jackalope is Texas' Loch Ness monster—rarely seen, frequently dismissed as a hoax, and yet perennially appealing to the popular imagination. Sightings are few, but the elusive creature is recognizable to most native Texans from postcards, on which an artist's rendering or the actual rare photograph depicts the rabbitlike critter in all his antlered glory.

There are many theories—all undocumented—as to the origin of the jackalope. One that has rarely received the audience it deserves is that of the mutant Aggie-experiment escapee. Sometime during the fifties, a battery of A&M scientists attempted to cross a jackrabbit with a deer, antelope, or elk, to provide an animal that would reproduce quickly and be equally suited for the purposes of hunting, eating, or transportation. The first attempt, between an elk and a hare (producing the stillborn hoppity wapiti) failed, but the second succeeded, to the delight of the Aggie team.

Alas, their joy was short-lived. Within months the first and only crossbred jackalope escaped from his Aggie creators and vanished into the wilds of Central Texas. Though A&M sent out scores of searchers from its renowned Corps, they were unable to recover the unique creature. Only then did the scientists discover that they had mistakenly transplanted into the bunny-cum-deer both sex organs, rendering it hermaphroditic. Thus the jackalope was able to reproduce in the wild, accounting for occasional sightings long after the estimated life of the grandparent of them all.

Another minor joke on the Aggies: They misnamed the creature, which is indisputably a cross between a jackrabbit and a white-tailed deer. Strictly speaking, the varmint should have been labeled a jackahorn, jackadeer, or perhaps even a bunny-buck, but not a jackalope. Its antlers are the slender, many-branched horns of the deer, not the thicker, stubbier variety of the pronghorn antelope, which, unlike the deer, does not occur statewide.

A second unproved theory of the creation of the jackalope is that the animal is indigenous to Oklahoma or Arkansas, where agricultural trendsetters tried for the first time to crossbreed a plant and an animal. According to this version, the successful hybrid combined characteristics of a jackass and a cantaloupe. This theory alone proves that the jackalope is a native of Texas, for only this state could come up with such a tall tale as the jackalope, a mythical creature only to be believed in by some donkey with melon for brains.

Jackrabbit

A jackrabbit—so called whether male or female—is not really a rabbit. It is a hare, which differs from a rabbit in that it is larger, boasts elongated ears, displays a different burrowing style, produces furry, as opposed to hairless, young, and has a flatter, less fluffy tail. However, the distinction between the two is important mainly to biologists. To the layman the use of the term "rabbit" is as acceptable as the use of the equally erroneous "sunrise."

There is only one species of jackrabbit (genus *Lepus*) in Texas, famed for its long ears, powerful hind legs, and amazing speed. It appears everywhere but East Texas. The state's only true bunny is the cottontail (genus *Sylvilagus*), of which there are three varieties.

"Jackrabbit" is a verb as well as a noun, meaning to move in a series of jerky hops (a description quite unsuited to the smooth, fleet motion of the animal). It is often used by rural driving instructors describing a high school student's attempt to learn how to shift gears.

Jalapeño

The medium-sized, dark green jalapeño is famed for adding spice to Mexican food, but it is by no means the only chile or even the only hot chile used in Mexican cooking. Other common varieties of chiles, or hot peppers, include the serrano and the poblano. The serrano is a paler green chile usually smaller than the jalapeño and also usually hotter, and the poblano is a larger, bright to dark green, roughly triangular pepper that ranges from hot to quite mild. (In some areas of Mexico the word "poblano" refers to several fresh chiles that are different altogether.) Poblanos are roasted and peeled before being used in Mexican dishes, such as the *chile rellenos*—stuffed chiles—for which they are a staple.

Besides the basic jalapeño, serrano, and poblano peppers, there are dozens more used in Tex-Mex and Mexican cooking (Mexico has at least a hundred varieties, ranging from bland to infernal and from white to almost black in color). All of them belong to the genus *Capsicum,* and many of them are better known dried than fresh. However, many types of well-known dried chiles are really one of the three basic Mexican hot peppers in disguise. Chile ancho, for example, is the dried poblano, and *chipotle* is usually jalapeño, dried by smoking.

Chiles of any variety may vary in their degree of spiciness from one crop to the next, but peppers from the same plant may also have various degrees of picante.

It is true that the seeds and veins of a chile are hotter than the flesh.

Javelina

Texas' bristly, betusked wild pigs, known elsewhere as peccary, are often reputed to charge hapless hunters deliberately. In fact, they are no braver than other nonpredatory wildlife. Their alleged fierceness is attributable to poor eyesight. Often they spot a hazy shape some distance away and rush up to it to get a better look—an action that humans, if the target, understandably interpret as a hostile charge.

Some critters erroneously called javelina are actually feral hogs, descendents of a once-domesticated pig gone wild.

Jeans

The Texan's uniform, jeans get their name from Gene, the Middle English name for Genoa, Italy, which produced a strong twilled cotton fabric called gene fustian. Jeans are no longer made of gene fustian, however; they are made of denim, which is short for "serge de Nîmes," after the city in France that produced a similar durable cotton cloth, usually blue.

Jeans have been popular in Texas since they were first produced by Levi Strauss and Company in 1850. The manufacturer of Levis, though, is not in Texas but in California—San Francisco to be exact. Early cowboys, always ones to appreciate quality, immediately fell for the thick, sturdy cloth reinforced with copper rivets. Soon they referred to all jeans or denim pants as Levis, a practice that modern Texans continue, though the Wrangler and Lee brands are also highly popular. Our ancestors would have split their sides at the idea of designer jeans. Today, however, even rural Texans adopt the fashionable names favored by their city counterparts instead of the good old standby brands.

Ranching rumor has it that the way a man tucks his jeans into his boots is a subtle indicator of the number of head of cattle he runs—say, the inside of the jean legs tucked in represents a certain amount, and the outside tucked in represents a certain amount more (despite the prevalence of the legend, few versions feature specifics). Though many ranchers and cowboys are aware of the legend, few accept it or apply it to themselves. Most of those questioned about the practice seemed to think that any fellow whose jeans were tucked, in whatever way, into his boots either got dressed in a hurry or was showing off a new pair of Tony Lamas. Most working cowboys and ranchers seldom wear their jeans any way but pulled down over their boots.

Jerky

Also called jerked beef, jerky is in no way jerked, pulled, tugged, or otherwise manhandled. Cowboys, with their less than fine ear for the Spanish language, heard "jerky" in the word "*charqui*" (or "*charque*"), meaning meat that is thinly sliced, peppered, and heavily salted, and then slowly dried in the sun. To jerk meat came, by backformation, to mean to use that method of preparing and preserving it.

Jerky is usually beef but sometimes venison and rarely any other meat. Because it was portable, long-lasting, unspoilable, and sustaining, it was—and is—a perfect trail food. It's also delicious.

Jersey Lilly

See **Bean, Judge Roy.**

Johnson, Lady Bird

Texas' all-time First Lady, she was christened Claudia Alta Taylor. "Lady Bird" is a nickname given her by her childhood nurse, Alice Tittle, who said of the infant Claudia, "Why, she looks just like a little lady bird!"

See also **Johnson, Lyndon Baines.**

Johnson, Lyndon Baines

The first and only full-fledged Texan to become president of the United States, LBJ embodied as well as reinforced the myth of the tall Texan. He owned a ranch, drove a Lincoln, wore a Stetson, and spoke with a drawl. Most of the tales about him and his presidency are not misinformation but the gospel truth. He invited West German chancellor Ludwig Erhard to a Texas barbecue at which a high school chorus sang "Deep in the Heart of Texas" in German. He hiked up his shirt to show reporters his gall-bladder surgery scar. He invited a Pakistani camel driver to visit him in the White House. He picked up one of his beagles, Him, by the ears and chuckled at the ensuing flap from dog and people alike. (The duo Him and Her weren't the only Johnson canines. Two others were a collie named Blanco and a Heinz 57 breed named Yuki, who the president always said was his favorite.)

However, a few stories about LBJ bear examination—first of all, the story behind one of his many nicknames, "Landslide Lyndon." The epithet arose after Johnson beat former Texas governor Coke R. Stevenson in the U.S. Senate race in 1948, but its meaning is ironic. Johnson edged by Stevenson with a mere 87 votes—and that *after* the Texas Election Bureau had declared Stevenson the winner. Almost a week after the polls had closed, election officials in Jim Wells County (not Duval County) rechecked their returns and found, in the so-called Box 13, 203 uncounted votes, all but one for Johnson. That particular county was in the domain of political boss George Parr, the so-called Duke of Duval, whose family had long controlled Duval and surrounding counties. Parr was an LBJ backer, and the list from his faithful subject Jim Wells County showed, remarkably enough, that the voters had signed their names in alphabetical order and in similar handwriting. The infamous Box 13 gave the winning margin, however slender, to Johnson, and despite a lawsuit filed by Stevenson that ended up in the U.S. Supreme Court, Landslide Lyndon prevailed. The rest is history.

After John F. Kennedy was assassinated in Dallas on November 22, 1963, Lyndon Baines Johnson was sworn in as the thirty-sixth president of the United States while aboard *Air Force One*, the chief executive's plane. However, the plane was not in the air at the time; it was on the ground at Love Field. See **Kennedy, John F., assassination of.**

A final bit of information about Lyndon Johnson: he did not coin the phrase "the Great Society," which he used to describe the American utopia he envisioned. Johnson's Great Society meant ironclad civil rights, an all-out war on poverty, federally aided educational opportunities, and a protected environment, among other things, but the phrase itself came from the title of a book by Graham Wallas, published in 1920 and referring to a society so great—i.e., powerful—that it subverted the rights of individuals to its own interests.

Joiner, Dad

Wildcatter Columbus Marion Joiner discovered, in 1930, the gargantuan East Texas Oil Field, sparking the wildest boom in Texas history. His nickname, "Dad," referred to his age—he was seventy when his famous well came in—though some sources suggest that he was called Dad because he fathered the East Texas boom.

The well that introduced what was, at that time, the largest oil field in the world was not the first well Joiner drilled. It was the third, the Daisy Bradford Number 3, named after the woman who leased him the land.

Dad Joiner did not die on Skid Row. That misinformation arose because, first of all, Dad himself freely admitted that he was "flat broke" and heavily in debt at age 65—five years *before* he tapped the gigantic oil field. In addition, by the time he did pass away, he had lost nearly all of what was estimated to be a $3 million fortune. He had been named in some 150 lawsuits involving his leased East Texas lands—because he frequently oversold holdings and blithely promised royalties to anyone who helped him out—and lost a great deal of money to various claims and lawyers. On top of that, his first wife sued for divorce, asking for half his assets. He then remarried, and at his death in 1947, his widow and attorney described his estate as of "nominal value." So Dad Joiner wasn't rich when he died, but he wasn't busted, either.

Jordan, Barbara

With her deep voice and unforgettable presence, Barbara Jordan, in her relatively short career, left a permanent impression on the state and the nation alike. But Jordan was not the first black ever elected to the Texas Legislature. Many African-Americans served as representatives and senators during the period of Reconstruction until the turn of the century.

Barbara Jordan was not even the first black since that time to serve as a legislator. She was one of three elected in 1966, but the others, Curtis Graves, also from Houston, and Joe Lockridge, a Dallas representative, were members of the Texas House. Barbara Jordan was a state senator. She went on to win a seat in the U.S. House in 1972, becoming the first black woman from Texas ever to hold that post (and also the first black woman from the South). Most Americans recall her as the star of the Watergate hearings, during which she impressed her countrymen with her stirring oratory and unquestionable honesty. Today she is retired from politics and teaches at the Lyndon Baines Johnson School of Public Affairs.

Jumping bean

Also called Mexican jumping beans, the beans themselves don't really jump, and they aren't even true beans. They are the fruit of two types of shrubs of the spurge family, especially one found only in Mexico—hence the appellation Mexican jumping bean. The jumping is attributable to a small caterpillar, the larva of a moth, that bores into the beanlike fruit, eats up the inside flesh to make a cave for itself, and settles in to wait until it matures into a full-fledged moth. Thus the market value of the beans as a novelty depends on harvesting the fruit while the caterpillar is still inside.

Because the caterpillar attaches its web and itself to the inner wall of the bean, its movement can make the bean, when detached, wriggle and hop—particularly if the bean is warmed, say in the palm of a hand.

Juneteenth

Juneteenth is specifically June nineteenth, observed every year by Texas blacks to commemorate the date in 1865 when a major general of the Union Army landed in Galveston and first informed Texas slaves that they were, at last, free. The holiday's real name is Emancipation Day, though everyone in Texas, regardless of color, calls it Juneteenth. It is a legal holiday nowhere but Texas.

Kennedy, John F., assassination of

On November 22, 1963, at 12:30 p.m., President John Fitzgerald Kennedy was shot and killed while riding with his wife, Jacqueline, and then-governor John Connally and his wife, Nellie, in an open motorcade through Dallas' Dealey Plaza. He was rushed to Parkland Memorial Hospital, where he was pronounced dead. Within the day Lee Harvey Oswald, a one-time resident of the Soviet Union, was arrested and charged with having shot the president from a sixth-floor window of the **Texas School Book Depository,** where he worked. Two days after that, Oswald himself was shot to death by nightclub owner **Jack Ruby.**

Those are the basic facts of the nation's crime of the century, and they are perhaps the only undisputed facts of the whole affair. Nothing is more riddled with error, confusion, and misunderstanding than the assassination of John F. Kennedy. Though mental pictures remain as clear as they were twenty-plus years ago— Lyndon Johnson's shocked face as he is sworn in, Jackie's blood-spattered pink suit, Lee Harvey Oswald's final agonized expression—the evidence remains in question, more challenged now than it was in 1963.

Within a week of Kennedy's murder, his successor, **Lyndon Baines Johnson,** appointed a commission headed by Chief Justice Earl Warren to investigate and report on the assassination and subsequent events. Ten months later, the Warren Commission announced its findings: Lee Harvey Oswald had acted alone, and there had been no conspiracy to kill the president.

The commission's report raised as many questions as it answered. First, it concluded that a single bullet (quickly dubbed the Superbullet) injured both the president and Governor Connally, despite testimony from various doctors that it would be impossible for one bullet to follow such a trajectory. The commission also determined that the president, whose car had just passed the Texas School Book Depository, had been shot from behind, though film footage of the event clearly shows his head flung backward by the impact of the bullet. In addition, several witnesses said they heard shots and saw and smelled smoke from the direction of the so-called grassy knoll, which was closer to Kennedy, ahead of him, and to his right. Besides differing on the direction from which the shots were fired, doctors in Dallas and in Bethesda, Maryland, where an autopsy was later performed, disagreed on the number of the president's bullet wounds and on which were entrance wounds and which exit wounds.

Those discrepancies are merely the best-known of the entire assassination case. For a full and fascinating account of the errors and inconsistencies in the Warren Commission report and the investigation of the Kennedy murder, see David S. Lifton's *Best Evidence*.

"Kick over the traces"

The expression did not originally mean to erase or to destroy the evidence of something. Traces are straps connecting a horse or an ox to a wagon or similar vehicle. Hence, whatever its popular modern meaning, when an early Texan said a horse had kicked over the traces, he meant that the animal had stepped out of harness. In a broader sense the expression came to mean "quit working."

King Ranch

Though it is the king of Texas ranches, the King Ranch got its name not from its prestigious position in the annals of ranching history but from its founder, Richard King. His first land purchase of 15,500 acres in Nueces County in 1852 soon became the King Ranch, which today has 825,000 acres. The current owners are all related to Richard King, though most bear the surname Kleberg. In fact, it is not King but a Kleberg—Robert Justus Kleberg—who is regarded as the ranch's true patriarch.

Though the King Ranch is probably the best-known Texas ranch today, it is not the oldest or largest in Texas history. The Armstrong Ranch was founded about ten years before the King Ranch was, and many ranches, such as the **XIT** and the Charles Goodnight spreads, were considerably bigger.

The King Ranch brand does not show a crown, a scepter, or any other royal symbol, nor does it feature the letter *K*. It is, instead, the running W. According to Tom Lea's *The King Ranch*, the brand first appeared on an early purchase of cattle by King. He liked and kept the symbol, which was hard to alter, required only a single curved branding iron, and had a smooth, fluid appearance.

Besides romance and grandeur, the name of the King Ranch evokes wealth. The ranch runs 60,000 head of cattle, mostly the famous **Santa Gertrudis,** a Brahman-Shorthorn cross that the Klebergs developed. But the family's wealth did not come from livestock, from its 1,000 quarter horses, or from the racing stables that produced 1946 Triple Crown winner Assault and 1950 Kentucky Derby winner Middleground. The money comes from oil. In 1933, the Klebergs, facing a $3 million debt, openly courted oil companies. Humble Oil took them up on the offer, acquiring the biggest oil and gas lease in the country, and spent twelve years exploring and drilling dry holes before a wildcat well came in. By the fifties the company had successfully brought in more than 600 wells. The King Ranch was saved.

Today, the King Ranch also includes three operations outside Texas: its Kentucky thoroughbred headquarters, a Florida farming venture, and both ranching and farming businesses in Brazil.

A persistent myth about the King Ranch concerns the myriad of curious local children who, folklore has it, climb over the ranch's fences and vanish forever inside its vastness.

King's Highway

See **Camino Real.**

Kirby-Smith, Edmund

Always ones to find the braggadocio in any situation, Texans have always stated proudly that General Edmund Kirby-Smith, who was commander of Texas forces during the last half of the **Civil War,** was the last Confederate officer to surrender. That is true, but there's not much in it for Texans to brag about. First of all, Kirby-Smith wasn't from Texas but from Florida. Second, his command included not only Texas but the entire Trans-Mississippi Department, which also covered Louisiana, Arkansas, Missouri, and the Arizona and Indian territories. Finally, though Kirby-Smith refused to accept Robert E. Lee's surrender and urged his troops to continue fighting for the South, the men—disillusioned by the news of Appomattox and tired and homesick to boot—had all but thumbed their noses at him long before he signed papers officially turning over his command. He professed himself shocked and saddened by the desertions, looting, and general disorder of the fleeing rebels, witnessing much of it firsthand in Texas, where he at last accepted the inevitable and surrendered his Galveston post almost two months after Lee's surrender.

Ku Klux Klan

A secret society of Southern white men, it sprang up after the Civil War, conducting a campaign of violence and intimidation against Blacks and their champions. The Klan, whose curious name supposedly came from the Greek word for circle plus a misspelling of clan, was responsible for myriad dreadful acts, delighting most in the flogging and lynching of freed slaves.

Despite its prevalence after the Civil War, the Klan essentially did not exist from the 1870s, when it was outlawed by Congress, until around 1915. Reborn, it did not limit itself to Southern members; it spread nationwide and increased its targets to include Catholics, Jews, and Communists. Throughout the twenties the Klan was widely tolerated in Texas. During World War II the Klan again virtually disappeared but then reappeared in full force in the fifties.

The first syllable of the name is often erroneously pronounced "Klu."

Labor union

Traditionally Texas is strongly anti-union. Texans have always cherished their independence, and they dislike being told what to do, even by a union that represents their interests. The work ethic is deeply ingrained in Texas culture and is reflected in the state's right-to-work law, which guarantees nonunion workers the same wages and benefits as members and which bans the closed shop. Other Texas statutes deter organizing and regulate collective bargaining. Texas was also the first state to require unions to register with the secretary of state.

Despite its anti-union history, Texas had unions as early as 1838. In Galveston, the hotbed of Texas union activism in the nineteenth century, arose the powerful Screwmen's Benevolent Association, which from 1866 until 1914 represented a specialized sector of longshoremen who used a jackscrew in their work. It eventually merged with the International Longshoremen's Association. Later, in the twenties and thirties, as Texas' industrialization tried to catch up with the rest of the country, San Antonio became the state's unionizing hub. At various times railroad men, butchers, and garment workers, among other groups, staged strikes there, and in 1939 Emma Tenayuca, a Communist, undertook her famous attempt to organize the local pecan shellers. In 1918 the organization that is now the powerful Oil, Chemical, and Atomic Workers Union was established in Fort Worth. Today dozens of unions have managed to take root in Texas, such as the Communications Workers of America and machinists' and steelworkers' unions, each of which claims more than 25,000 members.

Ironically, one of labor's great martyrs came from Texas. Albert R. Parsons, an Alabama native who grew up here, was an anarchist who was one of seven men hanged in 1887 for their roles in the Haymarket riot in Chicago a year earlier. During a huge labor rally there, a bomb thrown by a participant killed a policeman and sparked a riot that ended with six more dead and dozens injured. Parsons' widow, Lucy Gonzalez, came from Waco. In 1905, she went on to help organize the radical Industrial Workers of the World, better known as the Wobblies.

Lakes

Though Texas is hardly a land of lakes, it does contain 5,700 reservoirs, the 200 biggest of them with storage capacities ranging from 5,000 acre-feet to more than 2.5 million acre-feet. Texas' better-known lakes include Lake Texoma, Lake Livingston, and the Sam Rayburn Reservoir. However, with one exception, all of Texas' major lakes are artificial—that is, man-made. Only Caddo Lake, which straddles Texas and Louisiana, was originally a natural lake, and even it has been enlarged by a dam on the Louisiana side.

Lamb

See **Sheep.**

Lamesa

The seat of Dawson County in West Texas, it gets its name from the Spanish *la mesa,* "the table," a reference to the flat tableland surrounding it. Don't make the mistake of mispronouncing the name, though; it's "la-MEE-sa."

Lariat

One name for a cowboy's rope, particularly when used to catch or corral horses, but borrowed from the Spanish *la reata,* "the lasso," from *reatar,* "to retie." Originally a lariat was a rope made specifically of horsehair, but later both hemp and leather were used.

La Salle

The man who gave the French their brief and questionable reign over Texas, explorer La Salle landed on the Texas coast in February 1685—entirely by accident. He never intended to claim Texas for France. Three years earlier he had sailed from Canada down the Mississippi and taken dibs on the rich land at the mouth of the river, naming it Louisiana in honor of his king. He went home a hero and soon determined to return and colonize the wilderness. But he ended up with more wilderness than he bargained for.

With four ships and a few hundred colonists, La Salle set out from France, bound again for the mouth of the Mississippi. However, his expedition overshot its intended goal and ended up somewhere in the vicinity of Matagorda Bay. He had already lost one ship to Spanish pirates, and shortly after their unfortunate landfall two others were wrecked. The captain of the fourth ship then hightailed it back to France, while La Salle opted to stay and make the best of a bad situation. He founded Fort St. Louis and ventured out a few times to search for the elusive Mississippi, but two years later bad weather, disease, hunger, and desperation had so affected his few surviving followers that they murdered him.

Incidentally, "La Salle" was the shortened form of the explorer's honorary title, "Sieur de la Salle." He was born Renê-Robert Cavelier and acquired the title of nobility as a reward for his discovery of Louisiana.

License plate

Since 1917, when the State of Texas first issued license plates for motor vehicles, the plates have borne, besides a combination of letters and numbers, the single word Texas. The plates have never been stamped with the phrase "The Lone Star State," though many other states do include their nicknames on their plates. The only additional words ever to appear on Texas plates were "Centennial" in 1936, "HemisFair" in 1968, and "Sesquicentennial 1836–1986" in 1985 and 1986. A legislative attempt in the early eighties to add the slogan "The Wildflower State" failed.

For decades Texas plates were black and white, with the exception of personalized plates, which changed color every year. An exception was sesquicentennial commemorative plates, which were red, white, and blue. The plates were reflectorized in 1969, and until 1975 they had to be changed every year. At that time the state began the sticker method of vehicle registration.

Lincoln, Abraham

Texas, a slave state, did not vote for Honest Abe in the 1860 presidential election, but not because he was an abolitionist, and not because he was a Republican, either. The state didn't go for Lincoln because his name did not appear on the Texas ballot at all. Of course, most Texans didn't like Lincoln anyway—some predicted that he would allow the blacks to subjugate the whites—and, even had he been listed, would have supported the states' rights man anyway.

Liquor

See **Dry county.**

Llano estacado

See **Staked Plains.**

Lone Star flag

Probably no symbol of Texas is more recognizable than its state flag, the red, white, and blue banner with its single white star. The field of white is always uppermost. The Texas flag appears not only on flagpoles but also in miniature, among other things, on napkins, belt buckles, stickers, fruitcake tins, furniture, envelopes, and the rear pockets of jeans. Even the State of Texas itself selected a design of the Lone Star flag as its official sesquicentennial symbol. But by doing so the state contradicted an act of its own Legislature in 1933, which specifically states that the Texas flag should never be used for any decorative purpose or for any form of advertising. Oops.

Texas has its very own flag pledge, adopted in 1965, which says simply, "Honor the Texas flag. I pledge allegiance to thee, Texas, one and indivisible." Thus the pledge contains an error, for Texas is, by its own choice, divisible. In its 1845 terms of annexation to the Union, Texas and the U.S. agreed that Texas would retain the right to subdivide into as many as four more states. It's doubtful that Texas ever will, but the possibility exists that someday we might live in the Five Star states.

See also **Secede, right to; Six Flags Over Texas.**

Lone Star State

Another name for Texas, as even non-Texans know, but "the Lone Star State" is not our only nickname. Some flash-in-the-pan epithets—usually introduced by newspaper editors, chauvinistic or not—include "the Banner State" (because of its tendency to carry the winning candidate in presidential elections) and "the Beef State" (a self-explanatory phrase). "The Blizzard State" is clearly an outdated choice and a particularly inept one, based more on Texas' fabled ill winds than its relatively rare snow. It's also obviously at odds with the more recent "Buckle of the Sunbelt." When, to the astonishment of the nation, showman P. T.

Barnum in 1882 exhibited an incredibly huge African elephant dubbed Jumbo, Americans seized on the funny-sounding word and began calling anything big "jumbo." Thus Texas was occasionally "the Jumbo State," too.

Longhorn

Texas' homegrown cow wasn't homegrown at all. Spanish explorers and missionaries, anxious about having plenty of food during their travels and travails, introduced cattle into Texas as early as the seventeenth century. There were several types: a black Castilian breed, noted for its ferocity, and lesser types of various builds and colors. These cattle interbred rapidly, and they and their descendants so took to Texas that within 300 years the wild bovine population numbered in the millions, enabling many men left at loose ends after the Civil War to turn to ranching for their livelihood. Tough, wiry, well able to subsist in a dry land of sparse vegetation, the Longhorns soon became known as Texas Longhorns, as wild as the state itself. In the era of trail drives Longhorns were often called simply Texans (and Texans were often called Longhorns).

But with the demise of the open range the Longhorn was doomed. Barbed wire allowed cowmen to breed their stock selectively, for characteristics such as beefiness. The scrawny Longhorn offered a relatively low percentage of meat on the hoof, being equipped with a lot of bone, hide, and hoof to withstand life in a tough land. Despite the victory of beef cattle, the Longhorn is not extinct. There are 110,000 head in the U.S. today, about half in Texas, where they are used predominantly as seed stock for cross-breeding.

Lost Bowie mine

See **Buried treasure.**

Lumber

See **Trees.**

Margarita

No one knows who created the margarita. Bartenders from Los Angeles, Tijuana, and Acapulco, among other places, have claimed credit for first mixing the concoction of tequila, lime juice, and triple sec. (Occasionally, outside the Southwest, a margarita recipe substitutes Cointreau for the triple sec.) Many stories credit the invention of the margarita to various San Antonians. Another tale is that of an El Paso bartender named Pancho Morales, who supposedly invented the drink by accident around 1942 when a female customer asked for a drink he had never heard of. Instead of admitting his ignorance, he faked it and named the highly pleasing result after her. The Morales story, with various points changed or embellished, is probably the most often quoted version of the origin of the margarita, but it is suspect if only because its approximate date, 1942, is roughly a decade later than that of most other stories.

The truth is that no one knows who first gave us the Tex-Mex drink that can range from a powerhouse of a punch to merely a fruit-flavored frappé. Nor does anyone know for certain who the original Margarita was—a girlfriend, a customer, or the owner of a cantina. The younger generation of Texans know the cocktail as a 'Rita, but they, like their elders, are just as ignorant of its birth. So don't believe whatever tales you hear of the first margarita. The truth is lost in the happy hours of time.

Martial law

An unpleasant phrase and a worse reality. Fortunately Texas was more often subject to marshal law. But at least three times in Texas history parts of the state have been under martial law.

During the Civil War, El Paso was occupied by Union soldiers, who also held other towns as far east as Fort Davis. Their presence discouraged the Confederates' designs on California. The ports of Galveston, Brownsville, and Sabine Pass were at various times taken by the Union Navy before being recaptured by the South.

After the Civil War came Reconstruction, which was, technically, a period of martial law for the whole of Texas.

Sixty years after Reconstruction, Texas was in the middle of an oil boom. The new industry spawned dozens of riotous, rakehell towns, among them Borger, which twice in its first three years of existence was placed under martial law by Governor Dan Moody. After two periods of rule by the Texas Rangers, who tolerated no corrupt law officers, drunk wildcatters, or opportunistic prostitutes, Borger finally cleaned up its act.

Maverick

Pure Texan, the word "maverick" today denotes a nonconformist, a loner, or a rebel, but in its original usage in the mid-nineteenth century, it specifically meant an unbranded cow. The term came from Samuel A. Maverick, a signer of the Texas Declaration of Independence, who owned a few hundred head of cattle that ran wild on Matagorda Island. He never got around to branding them; hence local cowmen began referring to unbranded animals as mavericks, which were readily identifiable among branded cattle. At the end of the Civil War, when four years of fighting had deprived the state of many ranchers and left the cattle industry in chaos, the term came into general use as the soldiers returned and discovered innumerable head of mavericks roaming free across Texas. Eventually, maverick became a verb as well, meaning to help one's self to motherless calves or otherwise unclaimed critters—to steal, in short, though the practice was widespread, even among neighboring ranchers on otherwise good terms with one another. Branding was de rigueur, and woe to him who scorned the tradition or was slow to implement the practice. A brand had to be registered; if it was not, the brand itself was also called a maverick.

However, the man who gave us the word was not a maverick at all. He was the original solid citizen. A lawyer, Samuel Maverick received his prototypical maverick herd in lieu of a debt. Knowing nothing at all about the cattle business, he chose to ignore the animals and never intended to go to the trouble of branding them. Thus he never refused to brand his cattle; he simply didn't want to. In the cattle business he was out of his element, preferring humans to cows and the city to the country. He went on to make his name as a member of the Republic's congress and the state's Legislature, but today we remember him for a far different reason.

Mesa

From the Spanish word for "table," it means an isolated hill with steep sides and a flat top like a table. It differs from a butte, which is also a small mountain standing alone, in that its summit is flatter, wider, and less rounded.

Mesquite

In a state of prickly, spiny, and downright hostile plants, the slender mesquite tree appears almost delicate. And yet it is the hardiest of them all, featuring, below its frail branches and small leaves, a ferocious root system that hogs any available water. The mesquite tree is the botanical version of the rabbit, multiplying amazingly fast. Mesquite beans, which are the tree's seeds packed in handy pods, are quite tasty; both domestic and wild animals eat them and then spread the seeds in their dung. The seeds can sprout after decades of just lying around. Farmers and ranchers try burning, uprooting, and spraying the pesky plant, but they just can't beat mesquite.

Postscript for citified or transplanted Texans who are curious about the similarity in sounds: mesquite has nothing to do with mosquitoes.

Mexia

The spelling is deceiving. The name of the town in east-central Texas is pronounced "muh-HAY-yuh."

Mexican

Texas has a long and embarrassing history of prejudice against almost anyone dark-skinned and dark-haired, and that prejudice is still apparent among many Anglo Texans who persist in calling certain other Texans Mexicans. Get this straight: a Mexican is a native of Mexico. A native of the United States who may, to the prejudiced eye, appear Mexican, is nevertheless an American. An American of Mexican descent is a Mexican American. If you are unsure of the ethnic affiliation of an American, say "Hispanic." Refrain from assuming the person in question is a Mexican American, as he or she may have ties to Puerto Rico, Nicaragua, Venezuela, or any other country in Central or South America.

Also, a person who speaks Spanish is not necessarily Spanish, any more than a person who speaks English is English.

Mexican jumping bean

See **Jumping bean.**

Mier Expedition

See **Black Bean Episode.**

Millionaire

Despite Texas' fabled tales of super-rich oilmen and entrepreneurs with private airstrips, diamond pinkie rings, and longhorn Cadillacs, New York and California regularly outrank Texas on the *Forbes* magazine list of the 400 wealthiest Americans. (And Texas' ranking has, in fact, declined over the past decade along with the fortunes of the oil industry.) However, plenty of colorful Texans still rank way up there.

On the 1994 list, entrepreneur and presidential wannabe H. Ross Perot is the number-one Texan, with an estimated fortune of $2.5 billion ($60 million of which he spent trying to snag the chief executive's job). Others who possess the $310 million minimum required to make the '94 rich list include members of two famous Texas oil families, the Fort Worth Basses and the Dallas Hunts; Austinite Michael Dell, of Dell Computer fame; personal-injury superlawyer Joseph Jamail of Houston; another Houstonian, Oveta Culp Hobby, publishing magnate and onetime Secretary of the U.S. Department of Health, Education, and Welfare; and wheelchair-bound octogenarian James Howard Marshall, also of Houston, who made headlines the same year by marrying former *Playboy* Playmate of the Year and Guess? model Anna Nicole Smith. Various other Texans on the list made their fortunes in less typically Texan ways, including airbag sales and flight-safety training.

Perhaps if plain-vanilla well-to-do folks were counted—those with merely a million or two—Texas still might out-rich the rest of the nation.

Minors

In Texas not all persons under 21 are considered minors. In general an 18-year-old is considered an adult—for one thing, he can vote, a right guaranteed by the Twenty-sixth Amendment to the U.S. Constitution—but the legal age limit varies for certain other acts or offenses. For example, a Texan must be 21 to buy or drink alcoholic beverages. He or she must be 16 and have passed a driver's education class to acquire a permanent driver's license.

At 17 a person charged with a crime must stand trial as an adult, and in some cases a 15- or 16-year-old can also be certified as an adult. (Children under 10, however, cannot be held criminally liable for anything.)

There is really no such thing as the "age of consent" for a Texas minor. It is against the law to participate in a sexual act with a person younger than 17 unless that person is your spouse, unless the child can be proved to have been promiscuous, or unless the sexual partner is roughly the same age as the child. With parental consent anyone aged 14 through 17 can obtain a marriage license—or at any age, if a court agrees that he or she should be married (for example, if a girl is pregnant). A teenager of 16 or 17 can even petition the court to be declared a genuine, full-fledged adult.

Miss America

Though it has a reputation for having beautiful women, Texas has not produced more Miss Americas than any other state. California girls beat out Texas belles, six winners to three. Ohio (five), Pennsylvania (five), and Michigan and Mississippi (four each) are also ahead of Texas, and Oklahoma, New York, Illinois, Minnesota, and Colorado have each produced as many pageant winners as the Lone Star State. Miss Texas, though, nearly always ends up in the top ten finalists, a tribute not so much to the beauty of the state's women as to the efficacy of the state pageant mill.

Female readers need not be told that Texas men are pretty darned good-looking, too.

Mistletoe

The famous Christmas kissing plant grows widely across Texas, where six other species of mistletoe (*Phoradendron*) also grow. However, the Texas plant, though it is called Christmas American mistletoe and has the requisite leathery green leaves and white berries, is not true mistletoe; that is found in Europe alone. (According to Celtic legend, druids considered mistletoe sacred, especially when it grew on oak trees.) In addition, for al!

its seasonal importance, mistletoe is actually a parasite. Its Greek name means "tree thief," and it can eventually choke and kill its host plant.

Mockingbird

It was named state bird by the Legislature in 1927 because it is found all over Texas and because, according to the resolution of the Senate, it is "a fighter for the protection of its home, falling if need be in its defense, like any true Texan." However, four other states also claim the mocker as their state bird. Thus, it is hardly unique to Texas, and as an official symbol leaves much to be desired. That feathered personality the roadrunner, which clever New Mexico claimed first, would be better. Even the buzzard would be an improvement, for giving us the typically Texan vignette of its ominous silhouette against a bright blue sky.

Moon landing

See **Armstrong, Neil.**

Mossler, Candace

She was not a murderess—at least, not in the eyes of the law. Regardless of how the public recalls the 1966 case, the blonde River Oaks matron, then 46, was acquitted of the murder of her multimillionaire husband, 23 years her senior, who was stabbed repeatedly by an intruder in his Miami, Florida, hotel room. Candy's showgirl past and curious relationship with her codefendant, her 24-year-old nephew, fueled wild rumors about conspiracy and murder for gain, but in the end the Florida jury believed the blonde bombshell—perhaps because of her persuasive trial lawyer, the colorful Percy Foreman of Houston.

Candy's next husband, this one considerably younger than she was, also met with an unfortunate accident, though he survived. One night in 1972, he somehow slipped and fell from the roof of their house, just outside Candy's third-floor bedroom window. They were soon divorced. Four years later, Candy died during a heavily drugged sleep.

Motto, state

See **State motto.**

Mountain oysters

Neither oysters nor from a mountain. The name is a euphemism for the fried testicles of a bull, considered a delicacy in many rural areas of Texas. An adventurous diner may also encounter calf fries, turkey fries, or rooster fries—polite, if misleading, terms that are far more acceptable on a menu than an accurate description would be.

Mourning dove

It's "mourning" with a *u*, not "morning," though that's most likely when you'll notice their call. The name comes from their sad, soft coo.

Movies

The Texas mystique has always served Hollywood well. Since the birth of filmmaking, innumerable movies—mostly westerns, of course—have been set in Texas and have relied for their romance and adventure upon the state and its history. The very name "Texas" in a title adds a certain flair that no other state can match. For decades films capitalized on the stereotypical Texan (*The First Texan, Texans Never Cry*), Texas places (*A Romance of the Rio Grande, In Old Amarillo*), and Texas allusions (*The Yellow Rose of Texas, Deep in the Heart of Texas*).

But before 1970 few movies set in Texas were filmed here. According to Texas film scholar Don Graham, the first Texas western was actually shot in Denmark in 1908. Lest there be any confusion about the setting, the movie bore the improbable title *Texas Tex.* Most Texas westerns—such as the series westerns of Roy Rogers, Gene Autry, and Tom Mix—were filmed at Hollywood studios in elaborate sets. (Roy's *Song of Texas* featured a shot of snow-capped mountains, the likes of which have never been seen south of Denver.) Many other movies about Texas were made elsewhere too: John Ford filmed *The Searchers* (1956) in Monument Valley, Utah; *Duel in the Sun* (1946) and *Red River* (1948) were shot in Arizona; the great oil saga *Boom Town* (1940) was produced at MGM's Hollywood studios. Some Texas-set moves were filmed not merely in other states but in other countries. *Viva Max!* (1969) was filmed partially in Italy, and *Days of Heaven* (1978) was made in Canada.

Of course, what film fanatics might call the Big Three of Texas movies, made before Hollywood rediscovered Texas in the seventies, were all set and filmed here: *Giant* (in Marfa in 1956), *The Alamo* (Brackettville, 1960), and *Hud* (Claude, 1963). At the time, they were exceptions to the rule, but since then about 400 other movies have also been set in the state, which now boasts a film commission as part of the governor's office. Five Texas movies that won one Academy Award or another are *The Last Picture Show* (1971), *Tender Mercies* (1981), *Terms of Endearment* (1983), *Places in the Heart* (1984), and *The Trip to Bountiful* (1985). More recent productions filmed in Texas include *The Good Old Boys*, *The Stars Fell on Henrietta*, *Curse of the Starving Class*, *A Perfect World*, *Reality Bites*, *Blue Sky*, *Bad Girls*, *Leap of Faith*, *Dazed and Confused*, *El Mariachi*, *What's Eating Gilbert Grape*, *Rush*, and *JFK*.

Today television productions also abound in the state. Series that regularly film here include *Walker, Texas Ranger*; *Barney & Friends*; *Ned Blessing*; and various episodes of *Rescue 911* and *Unsolved Mysteries*. (Texas' most venerable TV series by far, however, is *Austin City Limits*, filmed at that city's K-LRU studio since 1975.) Miniseries include *A Woman of Independent Means*; *Heaven and Hell* (Part III of *North and South*); and the phenomenally popular *Lonesome Dove*. In addition, dozens of performers have made music videos around the state, including Billy Ray Cyrus, the Crash Test Dummies, Genesis, REM, the Bellamy Brothers, Meat Loaf, Kenny G., and a host of loyal native Texans.

Incidentally, the winner of the first-ever Best Picture Oscar was filmed in Texas. *Wings*, a story about World War I pilots, was shot in 1927 around San Antonio, where much pioneering aviation occurred.

See also **Oscar; Texas Chainsaw Massacre.**

Mule

A mule is not the same thing as a donkey. It is the product of a male donkey and a mare. (Cross a jenny, or female donkey, with a stallion, and you get a hinny.) A donkey can also be called an ass, and a burro is simply a small donkey. (A small burro could also be a burrito, but referring to it as such might lead to confusion in Texas).

Despite belief to the contrary, mules can sometimes bear young. Though male mules are always sterile, a few female mules have been known to reproduce.

During the nineteenth century, Indians rarely attacked mule-driven wagons. They considered the mule both inedible, unlike the ox, and unrideable, unlike the horse.

Murder

It has never been legal in Texas to shoot your wife's paramour, even in flagrante delicto—a common misconception fueled by folklore. No statute specifically permits such an act, but until women's rights began to equalize the status of wives, juries tended to view such crimes as justifiable homicide—after all, the victim was trespassing on personal property, and as a motive revenge has always served Texans well. In 1922, a Dallas man who emasculated, but did not kill, his wife's lover was convicted of aggravated assault. He appealed, pointing to the good old Texas tradition of allowing a man to redeem his honor, to which the court replied, in essence, that in that case he should have killed the guy.

Mustang

Not just a horse but a wild horse, and even more specifically a wild horse of the southwest plains that is descended from the original herd of Spanish ponies brought by early explorers to Mexico. Some equine fanciers say a mustang is only a purebred descendant, others that it is any wild horse. The name comes from the Spanish word *mesta*, which means both a roundup and an early organization of livestock owners; their strays came to be called *mesteños*, from which came "mustang."

Mustangs were the equine equivalent of Longhorns: tough, feisty, hard to catch. They were also highly unpredictable; thus cowboys came to call broncos or unbroken horses "mustangs" as well.

As a verb, "mustang" means to trap or hunt mustangs. As an adjective, it means wild, as in mustang grapes.

Navy

See **Texas Navy.**

Neri, Felipe Enrique

See **Bastrop, Baron de.**

Newspaper

The first newspaper in Texas was not in English but in Spanish—the two-page *Gaceta de Texas*, published in 1813. The first English-language paper came 22 years later. It was the *Telegraph and Texas Register*, the only paper to survive during the Texas Revolution.

Ney, Elisabet

Texas likes to claim the talented German-born sculptor as its own, though she was almost forty when she moved to the state in

1872. Her first name is frequently misspelled as "Elizabeth." Texans were outraged at her behavior. She treated her black employees as equals and also lived with a Scottish doctor, Edmund Montgomery, and bore two children by him. Although they were married, the artist always referred to herself as Miss Ney. She frankly enjoyed and encouraged her scandalous reputation, and though she was indeed eccentric, she was never as immoral as she wanted Texans to think.

Oil

The first use of petroleum in Texas was not as a fuel. Early Indians in East Texas used seepage from underground reservoirs as a cure-all for aches, burns, and cuts and also as caulking for their canoes. From them Spanish explorers as far back as the sixteenth century learned to use the oil as a lubricant for wagon wheels and axles. Even after the first successful **oil well** was drilled, the substance was still more likely to be used as a patent medicine or a lubricant than as a fuel. Not until the twentieth century did industries and railroads begin capitalizing on the value of oil and exploiting its use as a fuel.

See also **Gas; Hughes drill bit; Joiner, Dad; Spindletop.**

Oil well

The first oil well in the United States was not drilled in Texas. That honor belongs to Pennsylvania—Titusville, to be precise—where the event occurred in 1859. Seven years later one Lyne T.

Barret (often erroneously called Linus Barrett, or variations thereof) drilled the first oil well in Texas, at Melrose in Nacogdoches County. At the time the market for oil and related products was slim, and Barret could acquire no financial backing. Still, other entrepreneurs persevered long enough to give Nacogdoches County the additional distinction of having the first oil field, as well as a pipeline and a refinery that were somewhat, shall we say, crude.

Those early attempts were all short-lived. No commercially valuable discovery of oil occurred until 1894, when the city of Corsicana, drilling for water, struck a major reservoir of petroleum. This happy accident gave the industry its legitimate start. After the giant gusher came in at **Spindletop** seven years later, the Texas oil industry was on its way.

Okie

A person from Oklahoma, true, but the word "Okie" also means a migrant worker, particularly a picker of corn or cotton or any other crop. In typically snide Texas fashion, people in the Lone Star State also use the word to mean "hick." A fourth definition: to a cowman, an Okie is an animal of mixed breed.

Old Rip

Old Rip is the most famous **horny toad** in Texas. As local legend has it, he was placed inside the cornerstone of the Eastland County Courthouse when it was built in 1897. Thirty-one years later the courthouse was razed, and onlookers who swore they had witnessed the critter's entombment watched as he was extracted, sluggish but alive. Named after Rip van Winkle, he went on tour and was admired by thousands. When he died he was embalmed, and his desiccated little corpse—or what the locals say is his corpse—is on display at Eastland's current county courthouse.

As reptiles go, Old Rip is pretty lovable, but his story is also pretty hard to buy. Biologists, forever skeptical, refuse to accept the possibility that a horned lizard could live 31-plus years—five times the normal lifespan—without the sunlight reptiles must

121

have to survive and without a dependable and appropriate supply of food. Probably Old Rip is not so much an example of a superior horny toad as he is a superior Texan tall tale.

"One small step for man"

See **Armstrong, Neil.**

Oop, Alley

The famous caveman comic-strip character was inspired by Texas. He was not, however, intended to depict the state's residents as primitive club-wielders. Oil worker V. T. Hamlin, working in **Iraan** during a boom in the late twenties, was impressed by the stark, almost prehistoric terrain of the area. In his comic strip the characters Alley Oop and his girlfriend, Oola, share the spotlight with the tame Dinny the Dinosaur, an overlapping of man and beast that conveniently telescopes fifty million intervening years.

Oscar

Supposedly the bald-pated, gold-plated statuette, presented by the Academy of Motion Picture Arts and Sciences for cinematic excellence in the various sectors of moviedom, was named after a Texan, Oscar Pierce. Actually the statuette had gone nameless for four years when librarian Margaret Herrick, later to become executive secretary of the academy, reported for her first day's work there in 1931. A copy of the statuette was displayed in the academy offices, prompting Herrick to comment, "He reminds me of my uncle Oscar," or words to that effect. Unbeknownst to her, a journalist overheard the remark and reported the next day in his column that the Academy's employees had affectionately dubbed their famous statuette "Oscar." Herrick later admitted that there was no truth to her remark and that she had made it in jest—no doubt in an attack of first-day jitters.

At any rate, the statuette took its name from her uncle Oscar Pierce, who was not really her uncle at all but her mother's first cousin. Although he had at one time lived in Texas, where he was a farmer, when his famous namesake was christened he lived in California.

See also **Movies.**

Oswald, Lee Harvey

See **Kennedy, John F., assassination of; Ruby, Jack.**

Outlaw

To an early cowboy, not only a bad man but also a bad horse, one that was untamable or especially unruly.

See also **Billy the Kid; Hardin, John Wesley; Parker, Bonnie; Starr, Belle.**

Oval Office

The inner sanctum of the president of the United States, it is the nickname of his business office in the White House. However, a second Oval Office also exists. A replica of the room as it appeared during Lyndon B. Johnson's presidency is displayed in the LBJ Library in Austin, though it is slightly (one-eighth) smaller.

Oysters

Contrary to popular belief, it is perfectly safe to eat them in any month, not just those with an *r* in the name. However, the legal season for oysters in Texas, which produces as much as eight million pounds a year of the shellfish, is November 1 through April 30, which means they are harvested only in *r* months. You can still get fresh oysters the rest of the year, but they won't be native Texans.

Palestine, Texas

The East Texas town is named not for ancient Palestine but for Palestine, Illinois, the original home of a local pioneering clan. The last syllable of the town's name is pronounced "teen."

Panhandle

The Panhandle is not all flat, any more than Texas is all desert. The elevation of the northernmost region of Texas ranges from a minimum of 1,600 feet to a maximum of 4,600. Besides that, the presence of the Caprock, a looming escarpment produced by erosion, divides the Panhandle with a wall of steep cliffs, some of which, such as those in the Palo Duro Canyon, have sheer drops of 800 feet. North of the Caprock the Canadian River, which cuts across the top of the Panhandle, has carved out innumerable mesas and canyons, creating a tortuous terrain that is a far cry from flat.

Texans downstate are apt to breezily refer to any county up north as the Panhandle, much as anyplace out west is assumed to be **West**

Texas. The true Panhandle consists of only 26 counties, the northernmost block. Below those counties are the High Plains. Thus Lubbock, among other places, is not in the Panhandle.

Parker, Bonnie

The brave and glamorous heroine of Texas outlaw legend was neither brave nor glamorous. She had rather pinched features and facial scars, the result of burns in a 1933 car wreck. She was certainly not brave. Both she and Clyde Barrow, her paramour and partner, murdered not in self-defense but for enjoyment. History has tended to romanticize the famous Texas twosome, who in reality were cold-blooded killers.

Much of the popular image of Bonnie and Clyde—as a hounded couple forced into a life of crime and fighting to stay alive—is the result of Bonnie's own PR. She frequently left behind, in the remote cabins and campsites where they hid out, romantic poems that depicted the wanted couple as social underdogs driven to and resigned to their fate. Naturally, the newspapers ate up that kind of drivel, though they also reported the other side, the 14 or so pointless murders the two had committed in just over two years. Bonnie was also camera-happy, relishing dramatic gun-moll poses complete with cocked hip and drawn pistol. She later admitted that despite a widely circulated photo of her smoking a cigar, the image was all "bunk."

Bonnie was not married to Clyde. She had a husband, whose name was not Parker but Thornton and who was in prison when she and Clyde met. And although Clyde was a career criminal, with a history of juvenile delinquency, Bonnie had lived a crime-free, if rather wild, life until she met Clyde in the café where she worked as a waitress. She was 19 then; four years later, in 1934, she was dead, cut down with Clyde by almost 200 bullets fired from ambush by the Texas Rangers. Their violent deaths, however fitting, also reinforced the image of Bonnie and Clyde as a combination of hunted rabbits and Robin Hoods instead of a deadly duo who had reveled in terrorizing Texas.

Parker, Cynthia Ann

The state's most famous Indian captive, she was abducted by the Quahadi band of Comanche in 1836 during a raid on Parker's Fort, her family's isolated frontier outpost. At the time she was only nine years old. (Parker's Fort was not in West Texas, as modern Texans may assume, but in present Limestone County, in east-central Texas, which was then the frontier.) Her father and four other men were killed in the raid. She was not the only captive. Also kidnapped were an older girl, two cousins, and her six-year-old brother, John, who was never as famous as his sister, probably because the capture of a male did not suggest to the whites that most titillating of frontier topics: Indian rape.

Possibly the biggest myth surrounding Cynthia Ann Parker is that she wanted to return home. Young as she was, she adjusted swiftly to her new life, for all its early trauma, and soon forgot her white past. She married a chief, the famed and fierce Peta Nocona, and bore two sons, Pecos and Quanah. The latter, better known as **Quanah Parker,** grew up to become the war chief of the Comanche.

Cynthia Ann was not forgotten between her abduction and so-called rescue. Her story was known throughout Texas, and anyone dealing with the Comanche was always on the lookout for her. She was spotted at least twice before her final recapture. The first time a trader was unable to negotiate a deal for her return; the second, the girl, then known as Naduah, expressed her happiness with her Indian family and refused to leave. During a battle between the Comanche and a force of Texas frontiersmen in 1860, a soldier spotted her blonde (some say red) hair and saved her and her infant daughter from death. She was then 34, and though she recognized her white name, she suffered profoundly from her enforced reinstatement into what was, to her, enemy society. She was essentially kept prisoner, guarded and locked in a room to prevent her escape. When her little girl, Topsanah, died, she further horrified her white relatives by observing Indian mourning behavior—tearing out her hair, scarifying her breast—and refused to eat. She died soon afterward, of grief or starvation, depending on which you prefer to believe.

Cynthia Ann captured the imagination of the state and the nation. Hearts thrilled at the picture of a tragic woman returned, at long last, to the bosom of her loving family. But Cynthia Ann was not blissfully reunited with but torn away from those she considered her true family. In the 24 years since her abduction she had become an Indian. Like all returned captives, she excited sympathy, tears, and gossip, but her white family and neighbors were also shocked and angered by her refusal to embrace their ways. Whereas she had been assimilated into the Indian culture, she was an outcast in white society, if only because of what they considered her sexual ruination. It would have been impossible for the whites not to save one of their own from the "red devils," and yet, because they did so, the Comanche woman Naduah was doomed.

See also **Indians.**

Parker, Quanah

The famous half-breed is Texas' best-known Indian. He was the son of the chief Peta Nocona and the white captive **Cynthia Ann Parker.** His name wasn't really Quanah Parker; it was simply Quanah, which means "fragrance." White men appended his mother's last name, mostly because they took a perverse delight in the knowledge that the Comanche war chief renowned for his fierceness was half white himself. But Quanah, though he loved his mother and never denied his mixed blood, considered himself one hundred percent Indian. He certainly never spared an enemy whose race was the same as his mother's. In fact, his hatred of white men intensified because of what was, to him, the theft of his mother from her true home. He spurned the Medicine Lodge treaty of 1867, which sought to placate the Indians by assigning them a limited section of land they had once ruled, and from then on Quanah declared war on the white man. He deliberately invaded what was, according to the treaty, white man's land, and set out to murder the hunters and settlers he found there. His most famous attack, on a buffalo camp at Adobe Walls in the Texas Panhandle in 1874, was a failure. He and several hundred warriors were repulsed by a handful of sharpshooting hunters equipped with heavy-duty buffalo guns.

But Quanah was a realist. During the unrelenting Indian campaigns conducted by the U.S. Cavalry, he and his people held out as long as they could, but when it became apparent that they would never again be able to resume their traditional life on the plains, Quanah surrendered to save the starving remnants of his tribe. Once they settled onto the reservation, he continued as chief, often meeting with federal bureaucrats about tribal matters. Thus he became familiar to whites as a tame Indian, though had he gotten his way he would have slaughtered them all.

Quanah, however, was fully aware of white men's ways and, since he had no choice, was more than willing to take advantage of his new situation. He loved having his picture taken and wearing fancy clothes. He also loved shocking the whites with his Indian behavior—for instance, by taking eleven wives, to the dismay of local missionaries.

The white man's world almost killed Quanah, as it had killed his mother, and led to a final misunderstanding about the Comanche chief. In 1885 Quanah, with his uncle, Yellow Bear, was in Fort Worth on tribal business. They stayed, as befitted their stature, at a luxury hotel. The next morning Quanah was found unconscious and Yellow Bear dead because of fumes from the gas-powered lights. Whites assumed and their newspapers reported that the poor dumb Indians didn't know enough to turn off the gas and instead had blown out the flame, allowing the suffocating fumes to permeate the room. In truth, Quanah—who had survived only because he had slept near an open window—readily admitted that he knew how to turn off the jet but had simply failed to turn it off all the way. But white men of the era preferred the erroneous version; it suited their idea of Indian intelligence.

See also **Indians.**

"Pass the buck"

The buck in question is not a dollar bill, as you might assume, but a buck knife, so called because its handle was carved of buckhorn—that is, the antlers of a male deer. In the early days of the

West, gamblers kept track of who was the dealer in a poker game by passing a buck knife around the table. A player could opt to ante but not deal, and thus he passed the buck, meaning he passed the deal. Now the phrase means to avoid trouble by shifting responsibilities to someone else.

Pecan

See **Agriculture.**

Pecos Bill

Texas' greatest inventor, Pecos Bill (last name unknown) can claim credit for much of Texas' greatest symbols. Besides his obvious inventions—the lariat, the saddle, the six-shooter, the cowboy hat, not to mention whiskey—he also discovered rustling, rodeo, and train robbery. Ask any cowboy. Still, there are rampant errors in the various accounts of Texas' biggest, tallest, and most mendacious cowboy, whom a few disloyal Texans consider a fictional character. The mistakes are too numerous to consider in full, but a partial listing might serve to set the reader straight.

For example, one of Pecos Bill's most fabled feats was the riding of a cyclone. It wasn't a cyclone at all. It was a ferocious hurricane that, without his intervention, would have gone on to wreck the Texas coast more thoroughly than did the later Great Storm of 1900. As it was, he steered the storm all the way into Arizona, where he leapt off and allowed it to peter out, forming the Grand Canyon in the process.

Another of his better-known antics involved his girlfriend, Sluefoot Sue. Determined to ride Bill's wild-eyed bronc, Sue jumped on only to have the Widow Maker throw her off so quickly that she landed flat on her rear. Unfortunately (or fortunately, as the case may be) Sue was wearing a bustle, the springs of which were so powerful that she immediately rebounded high into the air. Gravity pulled her back down, and the bustle sent her up again, time after time. It is here that fact and fiction part ways. Legend has it that Bill shot her to prevent further misery. In fact, he roped her with his famous lasso, but her impetus was so great that she hauled Bill along with her and flung him right into the moon. He struck his head so hard that he let go of his rope, and Sue went flying out into space, never to be seen or heard from again, except by University of Texas astronomers.

Phillips, Bum

The former head coach of the Houston Oilers prefers being a Bum to being called by his real first name: Oail.

Pico de gallo

Similar to hot sauce but not the same thing, though the two Mexican garnishes share the same ingredients: jalapeños or other peppers, onion, garlic, tomato, lemon or lime juice, and occasionally cilantro or other herbs. Sometimes the *salsas* add cucumbers, radishes, and other vegetables. Pico de gallo—which in Spanish means "beak of the rooster," a reference to its bite—is usually prepared fresh, and the veggies used are left in chunks. Hot sauce, if not bottled, is usually prepared well in advance in large batches and chopped fine or pureed. Most hot sauces use pickled peppers.

Pierce, Shanghai

The famous South Texas cowman was christened Abel Head Pierce. He acquired his nickname when, as a young man of 20, he left the East Coast by stowing away on a schooner bound for Indianola, Texas. Discovered, he was shanghaied by the ship's crew into working for them for the rest of the voyage.

Plant

See **Bluebonnet; Cactus; Century plant; Indian blanket; Indian paintbrush; Mesquite; Mistletoe; Sage; Saguaro; Tumbleweed.**

Poll tax

It is a tax levied on a citizen before he may vote, and it is now illegal. But between 1902 and 1966, Texas had a poll tax, a requirement that effectively prevented many poor blacks from voting in elections. Though the poll tax is strongly associated with prejudice against blacks, however, it also discriminated against many Hispanics and whites who were also too poor to pay the voting fee.

Post, Texas

Not named for fenceposts, though there are plenty near the town, but for C. W. Post, the health enthusiast and cereal tycoon who gave the world Post Toasties. In 1906 Post moved from Battle Creek, Michigan, to the High Plains because of ill health. He purchased a quarter million acres and set up what he hoped would become a model city. He recruited hundreds of colonists, each one of whom he provided with a house on a low-interest loan. He built a sanatorium, as well as many other public buildings, and in his private little world indulged his fondness for experimentation. His most famous stunts revolved around rainmaking. He exploded dynamite at various sites around Post City, as it was then called, in an attempt to use shock waves to blast rain out of the clouds. He also worked with dryland farming techniques, unusual crops, and irrigation, but despite his many and varied experiments it is for breakfast cereal that the world remembers him today.

Prairie dog

The cute little critters aren't dogs at all but rodents with a puppylike bark and appeal. To farmers and ranchers they are a distinct pest. Their burrows can be huge. One in Deaf Smith County once covered 3,000 acres. Legend has it that at one time a single prairie dog town, some five miles wide, stretched all the way from Amarillo to Abilene, but alas, it had disappeared by 1900, before the varmint metropolis could be documented. Prairie dog colonies result in a considerable loss of grazeland, besides the incidental danger of the holes to livestock.

As early a 1903 the state permitted landowners to kill prairie dogs. Today it is still legal to use federally approved poisons or traps to do the job. Unfortunately for the prairie dogs, they

131

proved highly susceptible to poison, and their population plummeted in the fifties and sixties. Today they are making a comeback and still going far too strong to suit the landowners whose ground they ravage.

Occasionally you will hear that prairie dogs carry the bubonic plague. Far from being a myth, this is true. Prairie dogs contract the disease from a certain flea that transmits it from another infected animal, usually a rat but sometimes a bobcat or other larger animal. (Domestic cats are also highly susceptible.) If a human suffers from the plague, however, the threat of death is small, especially with the antibiotics available today, but the sickness wipes out prairie dogs. The disease spreads so rapidly that once a single animal has contracted it, the entire colony will be exterminated in a matter of days.

Urban prairie dog towns (a phrase that is not actually redundant), exist in Lubbock's Mackenzie Park and Sherwood Park in Odessa.

Prairie fire

One of the many dangers that threatened pioneer settlers, a prairie fire was more often caused by lightning than by human error. To Texas cooks, however, the term has a different meaning. "Prairie Fire" is the name that Neiman-Marcus culinary whiz **Helen Corbitt,** herself a pioneer of sorts, gave her refried-bean dip, a fiery combination of mashed beans, cheese, and jalapeños. See **Texas caviar.**

Prairie versus plains

The difference is grass. Both words apply to large expanses of land that is mostly level and virtually treeless. But "plains" refers more to the topography of the land, while "prairie" suggests vegetation, particularly tall grasses. Plains—or a plain, for that matter—can be bare, or if there is grass at all, it may appear only in short, scrubby tufts. Thus the High Plains contain huge areas of prairie as well as barer terrain, and the Coastal Plains, with their abundant and varied vegetation, include pine forests and desert as well as prairie.

President

See **Eisenhower, Dwight David; Johnson, Lyndon Baines; Kennedy, John F., assassination of; Lincoln, Abraham; Oval Office; Reagan, Ronald; White House.**

Prickly pear

See **Cactus.**

Pronghorn

Sometimes known as a pronghorn antelope, it is not an antelope. It resembles an antelope but is not related to any of the various species of true antelope. The pronghorn is a single species (*Antilocapra americana*), existing only on the prairies and plains of North America. Besides the pronged horns for which it is named, the animal is known for its speed. It is able to run up to forty miles an hour. It is also identifiable by the vividly white patch of fur on its rump.

Public lands

Sometimes it seems that Uncle Sam runs our lives to an absurd degree, but in at least one way his hold over Texas is considerably weaker than his presence in many other states. That's because, although the United States owns up to two thirds of the land of some Western states (such as Wyoming and Utah) it owns only two percent, 3.3 million acres, of Texas. When Texas was annexed in 1845, it kept all its public lands (as well as public debt) and the U.S. got none. Today the State of Texas still owns twice as much of Texas as the federal government does; however, most of its free lands were long ago given away to settlers or set aside for education funds. So when the wide open spaces of Texas beckon, remember, if you heed the call, that you're probably trespassing. Nearly all of the Lone Star State is in private hands.

Quick-draw artist

Not a fast caricaturist but a marksman skilled at the fast draw. However, the Old West quick-draw artist was not nearly as common as movies might lead you to believe. Though many gunfighters, such as Wild Bill Hickok, were widely and legitimately famed for their speed on the draw, that particular skill was not as highly prized as accuracy. Agility didn't keep you alive; accuracy did. The quick draw is practiced more today as a sport than it ever was in the nineteenth century as a method of self-defense.

See also **Gunfight.**

Quién Sabe

The historical Pecos County ranch, operated around the turn of the century, was renowned for its Spanish name, which means "Who knows?" However, the ranch did not have a question mark as its brand. It used as its symbol two overlapping half circles.

Supposedly the ranch got its name when a cowboy was asked what to call the brand—but who knows?

Today there is another Quién Sabe Ranch, headquartered in Channing, Texas, and owned by the R. H. and Joe Kirk Fulton families. The modern ranch uses as its brand an adaptation of the historical Quién Sabe brand.

Quirt

Yet another cowboy interpretation of a Spanish word, "quirt" comes from *cuarta*, a riding whip with a short stock and one or more lashes of rawhide.

Quitaque

The Panhandle town has a curious name with a curious pronunciation: KIT-a-kway.

Ranch

See **Four Sixes (6666); King Ranch; Quién Sabe; XIT.**

Ranger

See **Texas Ranger.**

Rattlesnake

Rattlesnakes, the American relatives of mambas and cobras, are the subject of as much misinformation as fear. First of all, rattlesnakes don't lay eggs; they bear live young (consider the expression "a nest of vipers"). Rattlers do not have bottom fangs, and the two fangs on top are not rigid. They fold backward out of the way until the snake is ready to strike. Rattlesnakes are usually three to four feet long as adults. Stories of ten-footers are just that—stories. (The record is under eight feet.)

Rattlers do not necessarily rattle before they strike. Also, the number of rattles isn't a reliable clue to a snake's age. It does not add a ring to its rattle for each year of its life. It adds one each time it sheds its skin, as many as four per year. However, a single rattle rarely contains more than eight or so rings. That is because the rattles grow brittle with age and break off on scrubby brush or rocks.

Texas has eight different species of rattlesnake, none of which is the sidewinder beloved of desert-scene illustrators. The western diamondback, Texas' most common rattler, is responsible for the largest number of fatal bites, though four other Texas rattlers are even more venomous. (The relatively mild-mannered coral snake is more venomous still.)

See also **Copperhead; Coral snake; Cottonmouth; Snakebite.**

Real names

Many famous Texans are known today by names other than the honest-to-God appellations on their birth certificates. Here is a list of famous native sons and daughters, and the real names they ditched for something deemed more fitting or melodious: Candy Barr—Juanita Dale Slusher; Vikki Carr—Florencía Bisenta de Casillas Martinez Cardona; Cyd Charisse—Tula Ellice Finklea; Joan Crawford—Lucille Fay LeSueur; Dale Evans—Frances Octavia Smith; Heloise II—Ponce Cruse Evans; Morgan Fairchild—Patsy Ann McClenny; Freddy Fender—Baldemar Huerta; Bessie Love—Juanita Horton; Meat Loaf—Marvin Lee Aday; Ann Miller—Lucy Ann Collier; Paula Prentiss—Paula Ragusa; Gale Storm—Josephine Cottle; the Alamo—Mission San Antonio de Valero.

Reconstruction

See **Civil War; Martial law.**

Red River

See **Boundaries of Texas.**

Refried beans

The pinto-bean mash beloved by Texans may be fried once, but the beans are not *re*fried. According to chef and food historian Diana Kennedy in *The Cuisines of Mexico*, the term "refried" is a mistranslation of the Spanish *refritos*. In that language the prefix "re" can convey emphasis or degree; thus *refritos* means "well-fried," not "refried." Though the beans are only fried once, they are often twice-cooked; first by stovetop simmering, second by reheating with oil in a skillet.

Refugio

Another Texas town pronunciation that you can't guess at—you have to *know*: it's "*Ruh-FYOOR-ree-oh.*" Substitute an *r* for the *g*.

Religion

At one time Texas had no freedom of religion. There was a state religion, which everyone was expected to embrace, and it was not Southern Baptist, as one might expect today, but Roman Catholic. In the early nineteenth century, when Texas was a territory of Mexico, the practice of Catholicism was a requirement for all colonists. The rule was, of course, impossible to enforce, and most Protestants merely paid lip service to the idea and continued to worship in their own faith. In Texas at that time there were few clergymen of any kind—Catholic or otherwise—and thus marriages went unsolemnized and children unchristened for years on end. (See **Cohabitation.**) When a priest did turn up at a settlement, there were often mass celebrations of weddings, baptisms, and other sacraments. Many colonists readily agreed to raise their children as Catholics only to insure that the kids would inherit their land.

See also **Baptist, Southern,**

"Remember the Alamo!"

The stirring battle cry at San Jacinto, "Remember the Alamo!" is usually attributed to General **Sam Houston,** the leader and best-known Texan there. The poor fellow who actually uttered the inspiring line was probably Lieutenant Colonel Sidney Sherman, who has long deserved the recognition, Sam Houston being plenty famous as it is. However, no documentation exists to wholly validate Sherman's claim. Also, the cry in full was not simply "Remember the Alamo!" but "Remember the Alamo! Remember Goliad!"—a reference to the **Goliad Massacre.**

See also **The Alamo.**

Republic of Texas

When Texas statesmen declared the Mexican territory a free and independent nation on March 2, 1836, they were by no means the first revolutionaries to declare Texas a republic; they were simply the first whose efforts eventually succeeded. Four other attempts to free all or part of Texas failed.

During Mexico's war for independence from Spain, a Mexican patriot named José Gutiérrez de Lara and a disillusioned West Pointer named Augustus Magee teamed up to invade and claim Texas for Mexico. They recruited the Republican Army of the North, took San Antonio, and in April 1813 declared Texas a republic. It lasted four months, when their troops suffered a hideous defeat at the hands of the Spanish army.

In June of 1819, a group of Americans—mostly Mississippians—proclaimed themselves disgruntled with the boundaries of the Louisiana Purchase as approved by the United States, which had renounced all claim to Texas. Led by James Long, the American expedition entered Texas from the east, marched to Nacogdoches, and declared the territory's independence. This republic lasted about as long as the Gutiérrez-Magee Expedition's. By November the Spanish had chased all the invaders back across the Sabine.

A third attempted republic lasted an even shorter time, less than two months. In December of 1826 a Texas colonist named Benjamin Edwards seized the Old Stone Fort in Nacogdoches and declared the Republic of Fredonia. He did so on behalf of his brother, Hayden Edwards, a local impresario whose tangles with the Mexican authorities had caused bad feelings on both sides. (It doesn't matter now, but Edwards was in the wrong, having used his position and power to bully and threaten other settlers.) Edwards and other Anglo leaders enlisted the aid of friendly Cherokees by promising the tribe half of the area of Texas. The

Indians' help never materialized, however, and by the end of January the Mexican Army had put down the Fredonian Rebellion. A fourth republic was not strictly Texan. It occurred when Texas was finally a full-fledged free state. Still, it involved some Texas territory and many Texas volunteers. In January 1840 a Mexican activist named Antonio Canales attempted to coalesce all the Northern Mexican states into a single Republic of the Rio Grande, with its capital at Laredo. Texas refused to get involved, and the Mexican Army readily overthrew the Rio Grande rebels.

Rice

Texans may prefer to eat mashed potatoes with their chicken-fried steak, but they prefer to grow rice. In 1992 Texas farmers harvested 351,000 acres of rice ($131 million worth); in comparison, the spud crop of 14,800 acres ($28.7 million worth) was definitely small potatoes. However, Texas does not rank number one in rice production. In 1986 it was fourth, after Arkansas, California, and Louisiana.

See **Agriculture.**

Rice University

Texas' premier private university, known for its stringent entrance requirements and usually unimpressive athletic teams, has been famous for years for having the highest campus suicide rate in the nation. Though the university—like many others—has had a few suicides since it opened its doors in 1912, Rice officials scoff at the idea that the college is as suicide-ridden as its students like to suggest—but then again no one is willing to deny it for the record.

Though still referred to as Rice Institute by longtime Houstonians, Rice has officially been "Rice University" since 1960. Though it was originally free to the lucky few who qualified as students, the university has charged tuition since 1965. Also, Rice was never a men-only school; women have attended since the very beginning.

Rio Grande

The name means "big river" in Spanish. Thus, saying "Rio Grande River" is redundant.

The river is also known as the Rio del Norte and Rio Bravo. It lives up to its name; it is the longest river in Texas and has the largest drainage area as well.

River

See **Boundaries of Texas; Colorado River; Rio Grande; Trinity River.**

Roadrunner

Also called the chaparral or paisano, the roadrunner is comical and endearing, if only for its inability to fly. In truth, it *can* fly, but not very far or very high. It much prefers to run, and many a motorist in Texas has accepted a roadrunner's invitation to drag. This feathered friend isn't really trying to outrace the car; it simply gets flustered by the alien machine and, because it runs better than it flies, takes off down the road.

Humans may find them lovable, but roadrunners are enemies to much of the natural world. Besides bugs and worms, they also kill and eat scorpions, tarantulas, and even mice. The story that roadrunners can kill rattlers is not only widespread but true. Behind that charming beep-beeping facade is the heart of a plains dweller as tough as the Comanche.

Rodeo

Although some sources give Canadian, Texas, as the site of the first rodeo ever, Pecos, Texas, can substantiate a claim five years earlier, in 1883. Two Arizona towns, Prescott and Payson, also claim to have hosted the first-ever cowboy sporting event. However, rodeos were a tradition of long standing on Mexican ranches, from which Texas cowboys borrowed the idea. The word "rodeo" was originally from a Spanish verb meaning to surround or round up, and what Mexican *charros* practiced as a natural outgrowth of their ranch duties their Texas counterparts turned into a no-holds-barred show-off contest. Many rodeo events today—such as roping and bronc busting—are obviously drawn from range work, while others like bull riding and steer wrestling were clearly added for the purposes of machismo and fun.

Texans cringe at the pronunciation of "rodeo" as "roe-DAY-oh," and yet that Yankeefied version is really closer to the original Spanish than our own "ROE-dee-oh."

Rogers, Roy

It's hard to believe that Cowboy Roy, like **John Wayne,** is not a Texan, but it's true. In Roy's case, at least, he married one. See **Evans, Dale.**

Rough Riders

Officially known as the First Regiment of U.S. Cavalry Volunteers, the Rough Riders were renowned for their exploits at San Juan Hill in the Spanish-American War. San Antonio cherishes its claim to the Rough Riders, and yet they did not come from the Alamo City. Organized by Theodore Roosevelt, the corps merely trained briefly in 1898 in San Antonio, always the most military of Texas cities. While in San Antonio, Roosevelt stayed at the Menger, the grande dame of that city's hotels; the Menger Bar now surrounds its patrons with Rough Rider memorabilia.

To correct another bit of Rough Rider misinformation: the regiment was commanded not by Teddy himself but by Leonard Wood.

Ruby, Jack

The Dallas nightclub owner never served any prison time for the shooting of Lee Harvey Oswald. He shot the alleged assassin of John F. Kennedy on November 24, 1963, two days after the president was shot, and was quickly convicted, in Dallas, of first-degree murder. Ruby (real name: Jake Rubinstein) remained in jail while awaiting a new trial with a change of venue, ordered by the Texas Court of Criminal Appeals. Before he could be retried, however, he died of lung cancer in 1967. See also **Kennedy, John F., assassination of.**

Rural population

Though Texas is widely perceived in the U.S. and elsewhere to be variously a wild, isolated, or hick place, it has been more urban than rural since about 1950, according to the U.S. Bureau of the Census. (The actual shift occurred just postwar.) Moreover, Texas today is more urban than the U.S. as a whole. Eighty percent of Texans live in cities or in towns of more than 2,500, whereas only 75 percent of Americans do.

Sage

Romantic as it sounds, cowboys cannot legitimately ride the purple sage. What is generally called purple sage (or sometimes Texas sage) is not true sage but a low-growing, flowering plant officially dubbed *Leucophyllum frutescens*—and it isn't common in cowboy country, to boot. Another pretender to the sage name is any of the small shrubs that dot the western U.S. and are widely referred to as sagebrush. In fact, those several species are grouped in the genus *Artemisia*. True sage, botanically speaking, is of the genus *Salvia*, which belongs in turn to the larger mint family and provides the popular aromatic herb used in stuffing and other foods. The faux sages, though fragrant, taste bitter and have no commercial applications.

There are also sages like J. Frank Dobie, but they aren't the botanical variety.

Incidentally, Zane Grey's classic western, *Riders of the Purple Sage*, takes place not in Texas but in Arizona.

Saguaro

The giant treelike cactus, with its stark, dramatic silhouette, is the ultimate desert symbol, much beloved of illustrators. Arms upraised, saguaro appears in multitudinous West Texas scenes, such as the illustration on the Old El Paso canned-goods label. And yet, though Texas can boast well over a hundred varieties of cactus, it contains no native saguaro. The giant succulent is found only farther west, in the Sonoran Desert of Arizona, as well as in adjacent areas of Mexico. Theft and urbanization, among other things, have endangered its existence. So, the next time you see saguaro on that Texas postcard or coffee cup, pity the poor artist who knew no better. See also **Cactus.**

San Angelo

Despite the masculine form of its name, the West Texas city was named for a woman. In 1867, when it was nothing more than a trading post, an early settler named it Santa Angela for his sister-in-law, a Mexican nun. Texans, always lazy about Spanish pronunciation, soon took to calling it San Angela. When the federal government established a post office in the city a few years later, authorities insisted on changing "Angela" to "Angelo" to properly follow the masculine "San."

San Antone

Certainly everyone in Texas knows what city you mean when you use it, but "San Antone" is not a widely used nickname for San Antonio, just as "Foat Wuth" is understood but not common in Texas.

San Jacinto

San Jacinto is both the decisive battle that won Texas its independence from Mexico and the actual battleground, located just east of Houston and now designated a state park. The site where Sam Houston's ragtag army bested the Mexicans is, to Texans, a shrine second only to **the Alamo.** However, in a way, Texans shouldn't be proud of the events at San Jacinto. Shouting

"Remember the Alamo!" a thousand or so revenge-seeking Texans took Santa Anna's troops by surprise and embarked on a slaughter, killing 630. The bloodlust of the battle lasted a mere 18 minutes. Afterward the Texans, still itching to kill, continued riding through the ranks of the fallen enemy, stabbing and shooting. The carnage was unnecessary if only because Houston's men caught the Mexicans off guard (they were concentrating on their afternoon siesta). Only nine Texans died.

The name "San Jacinto" is pronounced, Texas style, "san juh-SIN-toe." Spanish speakers who say "sahn huh-SEEN-toe" are technically correct but apt to be ridiculed.

See also **"Remember the Alamo!"** and **Santa Anna.**

Santa Anna

The leader of the enemy troops during the Texas Revolution, he was, at the time of the battles of the **Alamo** and **San Jacinto,** not only Mexico's top general but also its president. Santa Anna was a career military man, but he didn't believe in sharing the same harsh conditions his men endured. He traveled with a three-room tent and, in the middle of the Texas wilderness, comforted himself with supplies of opium, chocolates, and champagne.

Santa Anna was not killed during the battle, though half his men were. During the aftermath he was caught trying to escape, disguised as a common soldier. His expensive silk shirt—and the obeisance of his subordinates—gave him away. Legend has it that the success of the Texans at San Jacinto was due in part to his afternoon dalliance with a mulatto slave girl named Emily Morgan. (See **Yellow Rose of Texas.**) Thus distracted, he failed to anticipate the attack.

His name in full was Antonio López de Santa Anna, though he is rarely referred to as anything but Santa Anna.

Santa Gertrudis

The first truly Texan breed of cattle, Santa Gertrudis, like many stereotypical ranch dwellers, are big, beefy, and red. Produced about 1919 on the King Ranch, they were the first breed of cattle ever developed in the Western Hemisphere and the first new breed in the world in more than a century. By 1940 they had been recognized as a pure breed by the United States Department of Agriculture. However, the Brahman-Shorthorn cross was not named specifically for a saint but for the Spanish land grant that was the first property purchased by the founder of the **King Ranch.**

Savvy

As a noun, the word derives from the French *savoir*, "to know," and means common sense or know-how. As a verb, however, it comes from the Spanish *sabe*, "you know," and means to comprehend or understand.

Seal, State

See **State seal.**

Secede, right to

Texas does not have the right to secede, any more than any other state does. Which is not to say that Texas, or any other state, can't secede if it has a mind to; after all, 11 states did back in 1861. Many modern Texans have the vague idea—as did most secessionists—that because Texas entered as a former republic, it retained the right to leave the Union if it saw fit. However, no such clause appears in the congressional act authorizing Texas to join the Union. (See **Annexation of Texas.**) Because it was once independent, because it at one time did secede from the Union, and because its ideology is far different from that of the rest of the U.S., Texas has always clung to the idea of a guaranteed right of secession as a mark of its specialness and as a source of reassurance in case all else fails.

One privilege Texas does reserve, and a condition that appears in the resolution approving its statehood, is the option to subdivide itself into as many as four more states (a total of five). But Texas is more likely to leave the Union again than to fragment its identity and its land.

147

Seven Cities of Cibola.

See **Cibola, Seven Cities of.**

Sharpstown Scandal

See **Barnes, Ben.**

Sheep

Texas has always been predominantly a cattle state, and Texans have long had a bias against sheep. Historically cowmen and sheep ranchers were often bitter enemies, competing for the same range and water and despising what the other's stock did to the land. Even today sheep ranching has none of the glamour attached to the cattle business. Despite all that prejudice, Texas leads the nation not only in production of cattle but also of sheep—$111 million worth in 1992—as well as lambs, goats, wool, and mohair. Still, pro-beef Texans eat only one percent of the state's lamb. San Angelo is the nation's largest center for sheep and goats, and you can bet they know how to tell one from the other.

"Shoot the lights out"

What drunken cowboys did in saloons, no doubt, but the phrase had a different meaning to hunters. "Lights" is an old-fashioned expression for "lungs," so to shoot a buffalo's lights out was to shoot him in the lungs. The advantage of such a shot was that in case the bullet did not kill him at once, the animal's lungs would fill up with blood, preventing him from running too far to track down and skin.

Six Flags Over Texas

Although six different nations at one time ruled Texas—a figure that does not include any Indian nations—the actual number of flags that flew over Texas far exceeds six. It might be more accurate to say "*Twenty*-six flags over Texas." Though the exact numbers are negotiable, Spain and France flew one flag each;

Mexico, at least two; the Republic of Texas, at least two; the Confederate States of America, four; and the United States of America, probably 16.

Spain's castles-and-lions banner flew over Texas for a highly respectable 297 years, from 1519 through 1821, interrupted for a measly five years by France's extremely tenuous claim from 1685 to 1690, when its fleur-de-lis tricolor waved. While Mexico owned Texas, from 1821 till 1836, it flew two versions of its flag, the eagle-and-snake banner that is still used today and a tricolor emblazoned with the date 1824, a reference to the year of its most liberal constitution.

The **Republic of Texas** had two official flags. The first, a blue banner with a gold star in the center, was adopted in 1836. In 1839 the Texas Congress switched to the red, white, and blue Lone Star flag we fly today. In addition, 16 or so different flags flew over various parts of Texas before and during its revolution, including the **Come and Take It** flag of the first Republic of Texas and an assortment of flags alleged to have flown over the **Alamo.** (If those 16, though unofficial, are counted among the flags that have flown over Texas, the Texas total alone is 18, and the grand total 42.)

During the Civil War, the South adopted three different national flags—none of them the familiar Confederate banner that most Americans recognize. That fourth flag was actually the Confederacy's battle flag.

From 1846, when Texas officially entered the Union as the twenty-eighth state, through today, the United States has added 23 stars, each representing a state, to Old Glory, but on only 18 flags—because occasionally two or more states entered the Union at once. (By tradition, the star of a new state is added on the July Fourth following its admission to the Union.) Of the US.'s 18 flags, two—those adding the stars of Kansas and West Virginia—were changed during the Civil War and hence never flew over Texas or in any part of the Confederacy. Thus 16 different Old Glories, each with more stars than the last, have waved over the Lone Star state.

Some people doubt that existence of the 49-star flag. It did exist, however, and was the official U.S. flag for a year. Even though Alaska and Hawaii were admitted into the Union the same year, 1959, Alaska was admitted in January and Hawaii in August; thus their stars were added to the flag on successive July Fourths instead of the same day in that one year.

Six Flags Over Texas is, of course, the famous Texas amusement park as well as a reference to Texas history. For a brief time in 1965, it actually attracted more tourists than did the Alamo.

See also **Lone Star flag.**

Six-gun

See **Colt .45.**

Slavery

Slavery was not always legal in pre-Civil War Texas. When Texas was a territory of Mexico, slavery was frowned upon by the Mexican authorities, who recalled all too vividly their days of servitude under Spain. However, Stephen F. Austin, who never approved of the practice of slavery but understood the need for it, managed to persuade Mexico's leaders to allot his colonists an extra eighty acres of land for each slave they owned. (Mexico agreed but insisted that the children of such slaves be freed at age fourteen.) After 1822, Mexico made slavery illegal, period, though in Texas at least the rule was rarely enforced or observed.

During the earliest days of the Republic, because of Texas' agrarian economy, slavery was officially sanctioned in the new constitution—though it was never widespread, since most Texans could not afford slaves. Still, to throw a sop to England, which was a major market for Texas' cotton but was also strongly abolitionist, the constitution included a ban on slave-running. Thus slavery remained alive and all too well in Texas throughout the Civil War, until blacks across the state received welcome word of their emancipation in the summer of 1865.

See also **Civil War; Juneteenth.**

Smith, Deaf

In the callous manner of the day, Erastus Smith, a Texas patriot who fought at San Jacinto, was always identified by his handicap. But Deaf Smith never pronounced his first name "deef," as some Texans like to say it. That pronunciation is simply reverse chic. The county that was named for him also uses"deaf."

Smith, Edmund Kirby

See **Kirby-Smith, Edmund.**

Snake

See **Copperhead; Coral snake; Cottonmouth; Rattlesnake; Snakebite.**

Snakebite

There are myriad folk cures for poisonous snakebite, and all are complete bunk. Say you've been bitten by a rattlesnake. Would you accept a poultice of tobacco, garlic, or cow manure as your medical treatment? How about applying mud, a mixture of salt and kerosene, or wet tobacco?

According to J. Frank Dobie, in both Texas and Mexico exist stories of the efficacy of snakeweed or snakeroot, a wild herb that magically heals snakebite. But the plants are different in the different countries; in Texas the plant is a type of milkweed and in Mexico a member of the acanthus family. Both are medicinally worthless. An equally useless treatment is to apply the carcass of a freshly killed animal to the wound—ideally, the snake itself or, if he managed to escape, a chicken, rabbit, or whatever else is dispensable and handy.

The most common folk remedy for snakebite is naturally whiskey, probably less for its medicinal value than for its supposed ability to blunt the victim's memory and pain. In fact alcohol would more likely hurt than help the victim.

Today doctors are sharply divided on the best emergency treatment for snakebite. Often many forms of first aid that were once recommended are now recognized to cause as many problems as they solve. Tourniquets applied too tightly can further damage a limb; so can ice left on too long. The once touted cut-and-suck method is also out of favor with many physicians. The best single rule of thumb is to get a snakebite victim to an emergency room as quickly as possible.

See also **Copperhead; Coral snake; Cottonmouth; Rattlesnake.**

Song, State

See **"Texas, Our Texas."**

Southwest Conference

It is no more. After providing eighty years of gridiron thrills and chills, the Southwest Conference heard its death knell in 1994, when four of its schools—Baylor, Texas, Texas A&M, and Texas Tech—announced they would leave the SWC to join the Big Eight. That decision left the conference's remaining members—SMU, Rice, and the University of Houston—tackling their conference options. They had barely adjusted to the departure of the SWC's eighth member, the University of Arkansas, which bailed out in 1992.

Football fanatics may know that the SWC briefly included four other schools: Southwestern University, the University of Oklahoma, Oklahoma A&M (now Oklahoma State), and a third college in that state, Phillips University. All had withdrawn from the conference by 1920.

Spanish

Texas' second language, it gave cowboys—and the rest of us—dozens of words that we've never given back. Consider "loco," "stampede," "lasso," "corral," "ranch," "canyon," and "coyote." Can you imagine the **Alamo** by any other name? How about **chili, fajitas,** or **tequila?** Most of our borrowed Spanish sounds little like its mother tongue. Cowboys habitually mangled Spanish, so that most of those words don't reveal their heritage simply by pronunciation or sight.

See **Barbecue; Calaboose; Canadian River; Chaps; Frito; Hackamore; Hoosegow; Hurricane; Jerky; Lariat; Mesa; Mustang; Pico de gallo; Quirt; Rodeo; Savvy; Staked Plains; Tengallon hat.**

Spanish fever

See **Texas fever.**

Spindletop

Think Spindletop, and you think of the huge gusher that ushered in Texas' oil era. But wait: Spindletop was not the gusher at all but the entire field where, on January 10, 1901, one Anthony Lucas was drilling a wildcat well. Unexpectedly, at about 1,200 feet, the well came in with a tremendous roar, spewing oil hundreds of feet into the air. Christened the Lucas No. 1, the gusher blew for six days, losing an estimated 75,000 barrels of oil a day. Even after it was capped, the well's production had, within a month, exceeded Texas' total oil production for the previous year.

The Lucas No. 1 was by no means the first oil well in Texas. That distinction belongs to a well drilled 35 years earlier near Nacogdoches (see **Oil well**), which in turn came seven years after the first in the U.S.

Spindletop initiated an oil boom in Texas not because of the value of its oil —then only a few cents a barrel—or even because of the quantity it produced, but because of the newly discovered uses for oil as a fuel for industries and railroads.

See also **Oil.**

Staked Plains

The phrase, a translation of the Spanish *llano estacado*, denotes the area of the Great Plains in Texas that lies along the eastern border of New Mexico and extends inward and upward to the Panhandle. For decades most sources, using in translation the English word that most closely sounded like *estacado*, attributed the name to the wooden stakes that allegedly were driven into the ground by members of the Coronado expedition to serve as landmarks in the vast, empty plains. More recently historians have dismissed that theory in favor of a second, in which *llano estacado* properly translates as "palisaded plains" or "stockaded plains," a reference to the huge caprock escarpment that, in the trackless wastes, loomed up like a stockade. True, the story of the stakes is a bit more romantic, but it's probably hokum.

Starr, Belle

The beautiful heroine wasn't a Texan at all but a native of Missouri, and her pictures reveal a sullen, worn-faced woman of no particular charm. Yet Belle (real name: Myra Belle Shirley) must have had something to attract the dozens of men with whom she dallied, most of them criminals, such as Cole Younger of the famous outlaw family. According to her, she was married to many of her consorts—including Sam Starr, whose name she was using when she first achieved fame—and bore at least one illegitimate child. She participated willingly in, and showed a certain flair for, robbery, burglary, fencing, rustling, and arson. Though she was wanted for murder, she probably never committed one, but certainly abetted many of her murderous boyfriends or husbands. Like many outlaws who lived by the gun, Belle died by the gun as well. She was shot from ambush at age 41.

State bird

See **Mockingbird.**

State Capital

See **Capital of Texas.**

State Capitol

The Texas Capitol in Austin is not bigger than the U.S. Capitol in Washington, which has more square footage. However, it *is* taller; the Texas dome was deliberately made seven feet higher than that of the federal building (on which it is modeled), no doubt to give Texans one more thing to brag about. Besides that, the Texas Capitol is the largest of the state capitols.

The Capitol's exterior is composed almost entirely of the famous pink granite from Granite Mountain in Marble Falls. Early plans called for the dome to be constructed of the granite as well, but a structural engineer assured the builders that the base could not support the weight of the stone in the dome. Thus the very top of the Capitol is made of a steel framework covered with a skin of galvanized metal disguised to look like good old Marble Falls granite.

Texas' current Capitol is not its first but its fourth capitol building. The first two were temporary and were quickly out-grown. The third, a much larger and, the state hoped, permanent structure, was made of wood and burned to the ground in 1881. After that tragedy the Legislature arranged with an Illinois syndicate to exchange more than three million acres of Panhandle land for construction of a new capitol building. By 1888 Texas had a brand-new edifice of native pink granite, and the syndicate investors had the **XIT Ranch.**

In 1988 the State of Texas approved a $187 million restoration project for the capitol building ($5 million more was privately raised). Launched in 1990, the massive construction and remodeling job, which forced legislators from their offices and disappointed tourists galore, was the first ever for the Texas capitol and the largest ever undertaken for any state capitol in the U.S. The four-year project was overseen by the State Preservation Board, whose officials insisted on architectural and historical accuracy. Such tiny details as vintage fabrics and nineteenth-century cast-iron door hinges were painstakingly recreated to ensure that the new additions matched the century-old originals as closely as possible.

Note that "capitol," spelled with an "-ol," specifically means a building and not a city.

See also **Goddess of Liberty.**

State fair

See **Big Tex.**

State flower

See **Bluebonnet.**

State holiday

Texas has only five days that are true state (as opposed to national) holidays—that is, when state employees get a full day off. They are Martin Luther King's birthday (really January 15, but celebrated the third Monday in March); **Texas Independence Day** on March 2; San Jacinto Day on April 21 (alias Texas Sesquicentennial Day); **Juneteenth,** also known as Emancipation Day, on June 19; and Lyndon Johnson's birthday on August 27. (Other partial days off, real if not officially sanctioned, include Election Day, the secret half-day off for Christmas shopping, and the all-too-rare rumor-that-it's-going-to-snow day.)

Other days of great—or small—significance to the state's history are noted as special observance days—that is, they are important enough to be acknowledged by legislative say-so but not with a day off. Father of Texas Day (November 3) is Stephen F. Austin's birthday, but it doesn't rate as high as LBJ's. Sam Houston Day and Texas Flag Day both fall on Texas Independence Day, and as such get lost in the shuffle. The little-known Texas Pioneers' Day falls on August 12.

Some of Texas' special observance days are celebrated in many other states, like Arbor Day (third Friday in January), Poetry Day (October 15), and Casimir Pulaski Day (October 11). Who, you may well ask, is Casimir Pulaski? He was a Polish-born brigadier general who died in the American (not the Texan) Revolution. His day—the date he died—commemorates all brave "foreigners" who fought for America during the Revolutionary War.

See also **Thanksgiving day.**

State motto

Texas' state motto is not "the Lone Star State," which is its best-known nickname, but "Friendship." The motto comes from the alleged meaning of the world "Texas," though—if you want to get picky—the Caddo word that gave rise to the name meant "friends" or "allies," rather than "friendship."

State seal

It features an olive branch and a live oak branch framing a single gold star and surmounted by the words The State of Texas. However, there are no olive trees in Texas. The olive branch was chosen to symbolize peace, and the live oak, an indigenous tree, represents strength and fertility. The seal was adopted in 1836, having been inspired, so the story goes, by the design of a button (or cuff link or ring) that Sam Houston (or some other great Texan) used to impress a seal on the wax of an official document.

In the forties an astute but anonymous state worker discovered that the reproductions of the state seal then being used in state offices were inaccurate, portraying Spanish oak leaves instead of live oak leaves on one of the branches. The error may have existed since the adoption of the seal during the days of the Republic. Fortunately, the true seal, as depicted in marble on the rotunda floor of the Texas Capitol, correctly features live oak leaves.

The state seal has had a reverse design as of 1961, thanks to the concern of the Daughters of the Republic of Texas. Though the back side is rarely seen, it is a thickly and elaborately decorated shield that features the **"Come and Take It"** cannon as well as Vince's Bridge, destroyed by **Deaf Smith** during the Texas Revolution. These emblems are surrounded by the six flags of Texas, a gold lone star, more live oak and olive branches, and the mottoes "Remember the Alamo" and "Texas, One and Indivisible."

State song

See **"Texas, Our Texas,"**

State stone

It's palmwood, which you have never heard of because it is not at all common, even in Texas. A better choice might be llanite, a purply-pink stone that, although also rare, is found nowhere but Texas, in the geologically distinct Llano Uplift. Another choice would be Texas' best-known stone, the pink granite from Granite Mountain in Marble Falls, where the stone for the Capitol was quarried. It is reserved almost exclusively for the State of Texas' use.

Texas has, in addition to a state stone, a state gem, the topaz, which is also occasionally found in the Llano Uplift of Central Texas.

Steak

Though Texans are reputed to enjoy their beef nearly raw, the popularity of the rare steak is recent, postdating the practice of fattening cattle with grain. Historically, Texans ate well-done beef, because for Texas' first century or so, all cattle were range-fed—that is, they grazed on natural grasses—and as a result, the meat was gristly and chewy, requiring lots of cooking time.

See also **Chicken-fried steak.**

Steer versus bull

The difference is a big one. Steers are castrated; bulls are not. Nonetheless, Big Spring High School has the steer as its mascot. Cowboys, ever humorous, usually referred to steers as cows.

Stetson

The original cowboy hat, it is still the best-known of all Western headgear. But the Stetson is not a Texas invention. John Batterson Stetson manufactured the prototype at his Philadelphia firm in 1865, after a sojourn west during which he had yearned for just such a hat. His first design, called Boss of the Plains, was wide-brimmed and high-crowned to protect the wearer from the elements. It was immediately successful, and soon the Texas Rangers and every other man in cow country was not only wearing the hat but expanding on its uses: It could fan a fire, carry water to a horse, serve as a drinking cup, turn a jumpy cow, slash a slow horse, and just about anything else. Its flexibility allowed every owner to wear his hat at whatever angle he fancied and to shape it to suit his personality—upturned or downturned brim, round or creased crown, plain-banded or much decorated. Regardless of shape, however, probably the most memorable characteristic of any Stetson was its smell. Worn perhaps eighteen hours a day, usually in the sun, each hat became distinctively aromatic and sweat-stained.

So popular was the Stetson that soon any cowboy hat at all was called by that name, whether or not it was the genuine article (compare Levis, discussed under **Jeans**). Many a wearer, feeling downright friendly to the creator of his headgear, familiarly called it his John B. or J. B.

See also **Ten-gallon hat.**

Stone, state

See **State stone.**

Talk like a Texan

Not merely to talk with a twang or a drawl (see **Texas accent**) but, according to Western lexicographer Ramon Adams, to boast or brag. "Texan" is also listed as a synonym for braggart in some older editions of *Roget's Thesaurus*.

Tall Texan

The size of Texas as well as its rambunctious past led to the stereotype of the tall Texan—who, in addition to his unusual height, had plenty of grit and muscle to boot. Starting with **Sam Houston,** tall Texans people the state's history. It's hard to visualize a Texas Ranger, cowboy, or oilman as a Munchkin. However, there are scads of noteworthy Texans who were nowhere near tall, at least by Texas standards. Father of Texas **Stephen F. Austin,** oil well fire fighter Red Adair, wildcatter **Dad Joiner,** Heisman Trophy winner Davey O'Brien, war hero and movie star Audie Murphy, former governor William P. Clements, and billionaire philanthropist H. Ross Perot all measure in at five foot nine or under. And consider the women: **Ima Hogg** and **Bonnie Parker,** for example, were downright petite. Obviously what makes a Texan seem tall is not so much his actual height as his presence and pluck. See also **"Everything's big in Texas."**

Tank

Rural residents often water their livestock at a tank. Though that term conveys the image of a large, man-made receptacle, in fact a tank may simply be a plain ol' pond or pool. The common usage underscores the difference between a water supply designated for animals and one intended for human use.

Tarantula

They're big and hairy and they may give you the creeps, but tarantulas are not lethally poisonous (at least the Texas kind isn't; some South American species can, in fact, kill). The Texas spiders can and do bite, but the resulting wound is no worse than a bee sting. Even scarier than its bite potential are the tarantula's menacing, undulating walk and its tendency to leap several feet in the air when alarmed. But tarantulas are basically shy, preferring to hide out by day and emerge only in the security of darkness.

Tenderfoot

The word for greenhorn originally meant a cow, not a person. Today it can mean a newcomer or novice anywhere, though it implies that the recent arrival is in the West. "Pilgrim" also originally applied to cattle and not people—at least in the West.

Ten-gallon hat

There's no such thing. Imagine a cowboy hat the size of a kid's aquarium. Even a Texan couldn't go around with something that big on his head. A ten-gallon hat is merely a cowboy hat with a particularly high crown or a wider-than-usual brim.

The name, however, does not refer to the size of the hat. The "gallon" was originally the Spanish word *galón,* which means "braid" or "fringe." Cowboys, as usual wrecking the word, pronounced it "gallon" and used "ten-gallon hat" to mean one that was heavily decorated. Obviously it took a Texas-sized hat to contain those extra rows of froufrou, so quickly enough the term came to mean not an especially fancy hat but merely one that was bigger than average.

See also **Stetson.**

Tequila

Tequila is not the same as mescal. Both are produced from the fermented pulp of various agave plants—in the case of mescal, the maguey and in the case of tequila, generally a plant also called the tequila (*Agave tequilana*). Tequila is much more refined than mescal. (The raw spirit is called pulque.) In some cases tequila is redistilled mescal. In addition, mescal is nearly always colorless, whereas tequila, which takes its name from a small town in Jalisco, Mexico's chief tequila-producing state, can range from clear to shades of gold, depending on how long it has been aged.

"Mescal," originally from an Indian word, also means the mescal cactus. From the cactus come mescal buttons, which produce the hallucinogenic stimulant peyote and the derivative mescaline. The mountain laurel is sometimes called mescal bean because Indians ground up the plant's beans, which contain alkaloids similar to mescaline, and added the powder to mescal (the drink) to produce hallucinations.

Texaco

The name stands for "Texas Fuel Company," or at least it did originally, but Texaco doesn't live up to that name. Despite the regional connotation, Texaco maintains its international corporate headquarters not in Texas but in White Plains, New York. The headquarters of Texaco USA, however, is in Houston, and the Fortune 500 company (number nine in 1994) employs 6,000 Texans (32,000 worldwide), so it is still a Texas company at heart. The Texaco star was even inspired by Texas' Lone Star.

Texaco was created in 1902 in Beaumont in the wake of the **Spindletop** discovery. Unlike many Texas oil companies, it was never dominated by a single family. Its best-known founder, Joseph Cullinan, was not from Texas but from Pennsylvania. Its original board of directors was mostly Texans, four of them along with one New Yorker and two Chicagoans (including **barbed-wire** salesman Bet-a-Million Gates).

In 1985 a Houston jury decided that Texaco had illegally interfered with a plan by rival Pennzoil to acquire Getty Oil and awarded Pennzoil damages of $10.5 billion plus interest, a U.S. record. As a result Texaco, in 1987, sought protection from its creditors under Chapter 11 of the federal bankruptcy code, becoming the biggest company ever to do so.

Texan

A Texan is a native of Texas. Anyone born in Texas will always be a Texan, regardless of where else he might have been forced to grow up. As long as a person first saw light over Texas soil, Texas claims him or her as its own. For example, **Dwight David Eisenhower,** a native of Denison, moved to Kansas as a baby and always considered that state his home, but Texas claims him as a true-blue. Other celebrities who never made much of their Texanness are still proudly pointed to by Lone Star chauvinists: Joan Crawford, Carol Burnett, Meat Loaf, Steve Martin, Jerry Hall.

Texas has always had a tendency to appropriate whatever it desires, a tendency that long ago created trouble with Mexico and the United States, among others. Thus, if you live in Texas and contribute to its land or people a valuable service or gift, you too can be a Texan. (Any astronaut or athlete qualifies.) After all, from the very beginning the Republic and the state were populated with immigrants who meant to make good. Texas also tends to lay claim to anyone who passed through briefly but went on to fame and fortune: Walter Cronkite, for example, a UT grad.

Those early residents of Texas, by the way, were more often called Texians. Occasionally they might have used "Texican" as well, but by the end of the nineteenth century the residents had become Texans to all.

Texans are friendly

The state's name originally meant "friends," and the state motto is "Friendship," and yet the statement that all Texans are friendly is, like any generalization, false. Lots of Texans are frequently unfriendly to their fellow Texans, particularly those who live in the city instead of the country. In addition, once off familiar turf, many Texans forget to be friendly, perhaps because of their nervousness at being away from home or, more likely, because of their eagerness to impress the locals with the unbeatable virtues of their home state. An enumeration of Texas' virtues nearly always involves disparagement of the area visited, an unfortunate tendency that hardly endears the offenders to the locals' hearts. Ask any Alaskan or Coloradan.

Regardless of their behavior to their fellows or to beleaguered visitees, Texans are nearly always warm and welcoming to outsiders, no doubt to show them how lucky they are to be visiting such a friendly place, where life is much more definitely worth living than in whatever putative paradise they call home.

texas

That's not a typo. Without the capital letter, "texas" meant the deck of a steamboat on which officers' quarters were found. The various decks were named after states, and since the one containing the bigwigs' rooms was larger (as were the rooms themselves), it naturally became known as the texas deck. Today usually the texas is on the awning deck of a steamer and also contains the pilothouse.

Texas A&M University

It's not Texas Agricultural and Mechanical University. In fact, it's not "agricultural and mechanical" anything. By a vote of the Legislature the name was changed from "Agricultural and Mechanical College of Texas" to "Texas A&M University" in

1963. Obviously the letters still stand for "Agricultural and Mechanical," but that phrase is no longer part of its name.

See also **Aggies.**

Texas accent

There's no such thing. Because of Texas' size, because of its constant influx of immigrants, and because it has been influenced by both the South and the West, accents in Texas range from Southern drawls to Midwestern twangs, and many people in Texas, especially urban dwellers, have no particular accent at all. Probably the accent most widely considered Texan is the one at which most Texans cringe: the mealymouthed, grating pronunciation that sounds god-awful illiterate. The *g* falls off "ing" endings; "ain'ts" abound. President Lyndon Johnson had a particularly bad accent. His drawl ("Mah fella Amuricans") became the stereotyped Texas accent—though it also showed that people who talked that way weren't necessarily stupid.

Texas caviar

The Lone Star version of that luxury food is not even, say, catfish roe. The real answer is even more mundane: black-eyed peas, as first christened by Texas cooking pioneer **Helen Corbitt** in her heyday at Neiman-Marcus in the fifties. The original Texas caviar was a cold, spiced black-eyed pea salad, which Corbitt also made with garbanzos or red kidney beans. Occasionally today Texas caviar refers to jalapeño-stuffed olives.

Helen Corbitt also gave Texas its first official recipe of refried-bean dip. She combined mashed beans (she called for red beans, but pintos are better), cheese, jalapeño, onion, and garlic to make a spicy paste she dubbed Prairie Fire.

Texas Chainsaw Massacre

The famous gore film, the granddaddy of its genre, tells the blackly amusing story of a group of college kids who run afoul of a cannibalistic family hiding out in the quintessential haunted house. But the so-called Texas chainsaw massacre did not happen in Texas. The events of the movie were based extremely loosely on the dreadful exploits of a Wisconsin farmer named Ed Gein, who committed, among other pleasantries, grave-robbing, corpse mutilation, and necrophilia. The name "Texas" added a certain flair to the title that "Wisconsin" could not have provided. (See **Movies.**) The move was, however, filmed in Texas, in the country outside Austin, where the rickety farmhouse used as the ghouls' home still stands near Round Rock. A sequel, also set in Austin, was filmed in 1993.

Texas fever

It is nothing akin to the western craze that periodically sweeps the nation. Texas fever is a cattle disease transmitted by the cattle tick, which spreads a germ destructive to red blood cells. Despite the name, Texas cattle tick, which spreads a germ destructive to red blood cells. They, like all other Southern cattle, carried the disease but were also immune to it. The victims were Northern cattle, who of necessity mixed with their warmer-weather relatives at the end of a trail drive. The threat of Texas fever, also called Spanish fever, encouraged experimental cross-breeding by ranchers, who sought to develop hardy, disease-resistant strains, but Texas fever was also a major factor in the demise of the trail drive.

Texas flag

See **Lone Star flag; Six Flags Over Texas.**

Texas Independence Day

A Texas state holiday, it is March 2. The day, though it falls within the thirteen-day period of the siege of the Alamo, actually had nothing to do with that battle. It was, coincidentally, the day in 1836 that Texas' revolutionary provisional government declared the Mexican territory a free nation.

March 2 is also Texas Flag Day and Sam Houston Day, though these latter two are merely special observance days instead of legal holidays. See **State holiday.**

"Texas is heaven for men and dogs"

The oft-quoted and apparently sexist remark was not made by a man. Texas pioneer Noah Smithwick attributed the statement to an "old lady" in his 1899 memoirs, *The Evolution of a State, or, Recollections of Old Texas Days*. The exact quote, as he recalled it, was that Texas was a "heaven for men and dogs, but a hell for women and oxen." It is usually misquoted as "women and horses."

Texas leaguer

As any baseball fan knows, the Texas leaguer is a fly ball that falls too far out to be caught by an infielder and too close in to be caught by an outfielder. However, according to social historian and lexicographer Stuart Berg Flexner, the term did not originate as a Texas brag, though possibly the state's ballparks were large enough, or their hitters good enough, to make such flies common. Flexner traces the term to a minor-league game between Toledo and Syracuse in 1886, after which the disgruntled Syracuse pitcher complained that the three ex-Houston players on the Toledo team consistently hit what he called Texas leaguers after the equally minor Texas League.

The "Texas" in "Texas leaguer" can also be legitimately lower-case.

Texas lullaby

Not an actual song, though it is sometimes called "The Texas Lullaby," but a cattle call, the continuous, peculiar cooing and hooting that cowboys used to calm a restless herd of cattle.

Texas Navy

Curious as it may seem, Texas has had its own navy—and not just one but two. Both were established to protect its coastline during the days of the Republic.

The first navy consisted of a mere four ships; within two years, one was lost to the Mexican Navy, another was sold because the fledgling nation couldn't pay its repair bill, a third went aground, and the fourth was lost in a storm.

The second navy, also headquartered in Galveston, numbered six ships when it was commissioned in March 1839. Soon one was the subject of a mutiny and was subsequently lost at sea. Another was allowed to rot and was sold for scrap. The remainder of the fleet engaged in no particularly significant battles. The navy's commodore, Edwin Ward Moore, was accused by President Sam Houston of piracy, among other things. He was eventually vindicated. But the Texas navies were never what you might call a major factor in the history of the Republic.

"Texas, Our Texas"

Our pallid state song was written not by a native Texan but by an Englishman, William J. Marsh. He was living in Fort Worth at the time he wrote the music and, with native Texan Gladys Yoakum Wright, the words. Their combined efforts won a statewide contest sponsored by the Legislature in 1929 to find an original state song.

The lyrics as sung today are not those originally penned. The line "Biggest and grandest, withstanding every test" was changed by necessity in 1959, when Alaska entered the Union, to "Boldest and grandest, withstanding every test."

"Texas, Our Texas" is, to put it as kindly as possible, forgettable. Although **"The Eyes of Texas"** would clearly be objectionable to A&M alumni, among other Texans, "The Yellow Rose of Texas" and "Deep in the Heart of Texas" are two more logical and more likable contenders.

Texas Ranger

The original men in the white hats, Texas Rangers are the epitome of tough, tall Texans, Supposedly a Ranger could, according to a common expression of the day, "ride like a Mexican, track like a Comanche, shoot like a Kentuckian, and fight like the devil." And yet the Rangers were not always good guys. To Hispanics on either side of the Rio Grande, the Rangers were the terror of the border, known as *diablos tejanos*, "Texas devils." In the lawless wilderness that was early Texas, the Rangers were of necessity hard and cold, but they were often bloodthirsty and vengeful as well. The quickly gained a reputation as dangerous men and often used their position of power to avenge Texans' humiliations at the Alamo, at Goliad, and at the hands of the Mexicans in general. In the 1840s, just after the Mexican War, the murder of a Ranger in occupied Mexico City sparked eighty murders in reprisal. Zachary Taylor, then a general in the U.S. Army, for one despised the Rangers' unjustified killing of Mexicans. But to most Texans and Americans the Rangers were heroes. Their vendettas against "meskins" added to their glamour.

The harassment did not stop with the Mexican War. In 1875 a Ranger captain, Leander McNelly, took a force of men across the river to investigate a cattle theft. They descended upon the suspected town and wiped out all the grown men they could find. Then McNelly found he had attacked the wrong place. Unrepentant, he ordered his men to set out for the other rancho and repeat the deed.

An expression arose in Texas that summed up the Rangers' deadlines: "One riot, one Ranger," a testament to their skill and determination and to the fear and obedience they inspired. Despite the saying, Rangers rarely worked alone. They were at liberty to recruit their own men, and though frequently outnumbered, if not outdone, they knew better than to ride into battle alone.

Some Rangers went bad. Around the turn of the century, a Texas Ranger known as Killin' Jim Miller gave up legalized murder to become a professional gun slayer—a hit man, as it were. He made more money but, without the protection of the Ranger name, ended up dead himself in a few years, lynched.

During the border wars of 1915 to 1919, the Rangers ruined their own reputations. They persecuted hundreds of Hispanics—many of them native Texans—often indulging in torture before shooting their victims in cold blood. They burned border towns, including Piedras Negras. Soon the "Texas devils" had produced a new Tex-Mex word, *rinche*, a Hispanicized pronunciation that came to mean "bogeyman." Their actions became so reprehensible that soon the state legislature took action itself, limiting the force's power severely. Since then the Rangers have lived on in a force of only 87 statewide, under the jurisdiction of the Department of Public Safety. Their crimes are largely forgotten, but their white hats loom as large as ever to the nation's imagination. And besides, one of Texas' professional baseball teams proudly bears their name.

Texas Rangers are no longer solely male. In 1994, the agency named its first female agents ever, four of them.

Texas School Book Depository

The state's—and perhaps the country's—most notorious building did not start out life as a storeroom for schoolbooks, nor did the building ever belong to the State of Texas. In 1901 a farm implement company built it to replace another building that had burned. In 1950 the owners leased it to a private firm, also called the Texas School Book Depository, which still occupied it at the time of the **John F. Kennedy assassination.** Authorities determined that from a sixth-floor window of the building an employee, Lee Harvey Oswald, acting alone, fired a single shot that killed the president. That assertation is, of course, much disputed. The sixth floor was still padlocked when Dallas County bought the building in 1977 to use it for county offices. In 1989, the sixth floor became a museum dedicated to chronicling JFK's life and death.

Texas tea

Not a drink, even at the University of Texas, but a phrase meaning a different sort of liquid: oil.

Texas toast

You could maintain that "Here's to Texas," said while hoisting a cold Lone Star beer, is a Texas toast, but the better-known kind is really extra-thick bread that is not actually toasted but buttered and grilled. It is a staple trimming served by roadside cafés with chicken-fried steak and other regional dishes.

Texian

See **Texan.**

Tex-Mex

Lone Star shorthand, the phrase refers specifically to dishes that are part Texan, part Mexican in flavor, heritage, and evolution. No matter what the uninitiated may think, Tex-Mex food is not really very hot. That's why picante sauce always accompanies it, so that fire-eaters can spice up their own servings without burning fellow diners.

See **Burrito; Chili; Fajita; Hot sauce; Pico de gallo.**

Thanksgiving day

From 1939 through 1956, Texas observed Thanksgiving on a different day from the rest of the country—on the fifth Thursday of the month, if there was one, whereas the national day traditionally fell on the fourth Thursday. In 1957 the Legislature called a halt to the occasional double holiday and ordered that it coincide in all years with the national date.

See also **State holidays.**

Tidelands controversy

See **Boundaries of Texas.**

Tomb of the Unknown Soldier

Most Texans know the famous monument as part of the Arlington National Cemetery in Washington, D.C. However, Texas has its own Tomb of the Unknown Soldier—of the Indian wars—in Fort Worth's Pioneer Rest Cemetery.

Tornado

Though northeastern Texas contains the so-called Tornado Alley, of which Wichita Falls is the undisputed capital, Texas has not suffered tornadoes as frequently as has Oklahoma, where every year about eight occur in every ten thousand square miles. Only six per ten thousand occur in parts of Texas. However, Texas, because of its sheer size, has more tornadoes every year than any other state, usually around 125, most of them in Tornado Alley.

Civil defense authorities once advocated leaving doors and windows open during a tornado, to reduce the pressure within a house. Now they know it is safer to leave doors and windows closed. Another common myth is that you should try to escape a tornado in your car. Wrong. It is highly dangerous, and many victims of tornadoes thought their car meant salvation when in fact it turned into a death trap. It is also safer to be out in the open, taking cover in a ditch or gully, than to remain in a mobile home, which is even more dangerous than a car. Inside a sturdier structure, such as a house or office building, the safest place is in the storm cellar or basement, if there is one, or the smallest room with the fewest windows and doors.

Few Texans call a tornado anything but a tornado, though "cyclone" and "twister" are not uncommon. "Cyclone" once meant a hurricane as well.

See also **Hurricane; Weather.**

Trail drive

Nothing in Texas history can beat the sheer romance of the trail drive—the lowing cattle, the billowing dust, the hard-riding cowboys. Yet many myths about trail drives persist, more than a hundred years after their decline.

For one thing, the trail drive was quite a short-lived phenomenon, starting around 1866 and lasting only about twenty years. Cattle drives were never that major a force in Texas' economy, and only a tiny percentage of Texans—whether employer or employee—participated in them. The farmer, particularly the cotton farmer, was a much greater factor in the state for a much longer time, and yet farming simply cannot approach the drama, excitement, and power of the trail drive.

Most drives were rather low-key affairs, involving perhaps one thousand or two thousand head of cattle, a far cry from the trail drive of the movies, in which the camera pans a boiling, bawling, unending mass of steers. A trail drive needed one cowboy, or drover, for each two hundred to three hundred head.

The most important man on a trail drive wasn't the owner of the cattle or the foreman of the hands. He was the cook, and he received a higher wage to prove it. Good food was the only bright spot during the long hard days of the trail, and it could make the difference between a good and a bad trip. Despite the filth, the fatigue, the storms, and the stampedes, most cowboys who had gone up the trail remembered the experience as the best time of their lives.

Speaking of stampedes, they were most often caused by thunder and lightning. And contrary to Hollywood depictions, firing a gun to halt stampeding cattle was useless. Usually cowboys had to force the herd to turn or simply let the cattle run till they were winded or till something impeded their progress.

Not all cattle drives originated in Texas, though by far the majority did. Nor did all drives end up in Abilene or Dodge City, Kansas—some went as far north as Montana. But the Texas-to-Kansas routes, like the famous **Chisholm Trail,** were the ones most heavily traveled and the ones whose names still resound today.

See also **Texas fever.**

Travis, William Barret

The commander of the **Alamo** was no hero in private life. He abandoned his wife and two children in Alabama to come to Texas in the first place. Once here, he carried on with various young women—recording his conquests in a diary—and also apparently suffered from venereal disease. Still, he distinguished himself with his courageous, if hotheaded, behavior at Texas' Cradle of Liberty, which to most Texans is all that counts.

Treasure

See **Buried treasure.**

Treaty of Annexation

See **Annexation of Texas.**

Tree

Many non-Texans and Texans as well visualize much of the state as a treeless waste, empty of greenery. Wrong again. There are 150 species of trees in Texas (800 if you count bushes, shrubs, and similar woody plants). About 23 million acres in the state are forested, mostly in East Texas, where lumber has always been a big industry. In 1907 Texas was the number-three lumber-producing state. Since then it hasn't felled quite so many of its pines, but today it still ranks anywhere from sixth to eighth in timber production.

Trinity River

Although the Trinity has three main forks—the West, the East, and the Elm—that is not how the river got its name. In the late seventeenth century a traveling Spaniard christened it Rio de la Santisima Trinidad, or River of the Most Holy Trinity.

Tumbleweed

When it's growing, the plant is not a tumbleweed but a Russian thistle. Only when its thin stalk is broken off by the wind and it has become dry and brittle does the plant become a tumbleweed. This most evocative of Texas plants was not originally a Texan; it was imported accidentally in the 1870s in shipments of flaxseeds belonging to Russian settlers. Perhaps, some say, that is why the tumbleweed wanders—it's trying to find its way back home.

Two bits

Slang for a quarter, or twenty-five cents, the expression came from the Spanish colonial dollars called pieces of eight, because they contained eight reales, each of which was worth twelve and a half cents. Thus a dollar had eight bits, as the Texan put it, preferring to use that word rather than struggle to pronounce "reales." Texas folklore, however, has it that poor pioneers and frontiersmen hacked out pieces of a silver dollar to pay the nearest store or trading post, and those fragments of coin came to be known as bits.

University of Texas

Graduates of the Austin campus might disagree, but there is more than one University of Texas. The system has branches in Arlington, El Paso, the Permian Basin, San Antonio, and Tyler as well as its main campus in the capital. If you don't specify a location, however, then "University of Texas" or "UT" certainly refers to the Austin school, which is properly known as the University of Texas at Austin. Besides its colleges, the UT system also maintains health science centers or medical branches in Dallas, Galveston, Houston, San Antonio, and Tyler.

UT is known to many as Texas University. But actually the first Texas University was what is now Southwestern University in Georgetown. It bore that name for a year and a half until it was chartered in 1875.

See also **Hook 'em!**

Union

See **Labor Union.**

Valley

There are various valleys in Texas, but if someone refers simply to "the Valley," he means the Lower Rio Grande Valley, Texas' headquarters for citrus fruit and winter vegetables (as well as "snowbirds"—people, many of them senior citizens and Yankees, who come south for the milder winter).

Van Cliburn

See **Cliburn, Van.**

Villa, Pancho

His real name was Doroteo Arango. He was Mexican, born in the state of Durango, though he lived in El Paso for a few years beginning in 1913 and occasionally claimed American citizenship. He began life as a cattle rustler and took the name "Villa" from a local bandit in his native state. His career as a revolutionary was unintentional. A Latin Robin Hood, he divided the spoils of his various raids among the needy, and soon his popularity with the poor inspired him to greater deeds in the name of the people.

His most famous act was his attack on Columbus, New Mexico, in March of 1916. Because a detachment of the 13th U.S. Cavalry was stationed there, the U.S. government, outraged, considered it a military invasion, although the soldiers had successfully repelled Villa and the town itself suffered the brunt of the attack. President Woodrow Wilson ordered a punitive expedition led by General John J. Pershing (and participated in by a young George S. Patton). However, Villa made two later attacks on U.S. towns that went unpunished and virtually unnoticed because the settlements were much smaller and neither contained a military post. In May of 1916 Villa's army attacked Boquillas and Glen Spring (or Glenn Springs), two Big Bend villages on the Rio Grande. Looting of the general stores was the extent of the damage.

Though most of Villa's victims were killed in the name of revolution, he killed at least one man in cold blood, a wealthy landowner's son who had raped his sister—or so the story goes. He is remembered as a political hero, and yet there is no question that Villa was a criminal first and a revolutionary second.

See also **Cortinas, Juan.**

Vulture

See **Buzzard.**

Waco

Don't pronounce the town's name "Wacko," no matter what your opinion of its largely Baptist inhabitants. It's "*WAY-ko*."

War Between the States

See **Civil War.**

Wayne, John

Probably the most Texan Texan that ever lived wasn't a Texan at all. The Duke (real name: Marion Michael Morrison) was born May 26, 1907, in Winterset, Iowa. The quintessential cowboy was, however, an honorary Texas Ranger.

Weather

Weather in Texas is no more unpredictable than weather anywhere else—it's just that Texas' sheer size allows for both a variety in climate and extremes in temperature. Texas is nationally renowned for its heat—as much as 120 degrees Fahrenheit in the summer, a record set in Seymour in 1936—but not especially for its humidity, though a good half of Texas swelters in summer weather that is a far cry from the famed dryness of the Panhandle and West Texas. Parts of Texas get plenty of rain, such as Clarksville, which set a record of 109 inches in 1873. At the other extreme there's Wink, which registered only 1¼ inch in 1956. And although Texas is the buckle of the Sunbelt, it has suffered its share of cold. Various winter records include a low of 23 degrees below zero (Fahrenheit) at Tulia in 1899 and Seminole in 1933 and 24 inches of snow in 24 hours at Plainview in 1956.

See also **Dryness of Texas; Hurricane; Tornado.**

West Texas

The phrase is used by urban Texans and Texans east of the Colorado River to mean anything west of where they live. "West Texas" is a highly sketchy term, meaning, depending on whom you're talking to, anywhere from the Panhandle to El Paso to Big Bend or even farther down the Rio Grande. Half the state is West Texas to the other half. And because the western half is less populated and less well known, it is easier to use a vague term like "West Texas" instead of specifics like "Trans-Pecos" or "High Plains" or "Edwards Plateau."

Wet county

See **Dry county.**

Wheat

See **Agriculture.**

White House

The White House is not only in Washington, D.C. It is a Texas governor's mansion—but not *the* Texas Governor's Mansion. In La Porte, facing Galveston Bay, is the Texas White House, an exact replica of the U.S. president's home but only three-fifths the size. It was built by former governor Ross Sterling, who later donated it to charity.

Wildflower

See **Bluebonnet; Indian blanket; Indian paintbrush; Sage.**

Wine

The Texas industry that sprang up in the seventies and boomed in the eighties is not new. It is actually a continuation of a practice that is hundreds of years old. Spanish missionaries maintained vineyards as far back as the eighteenth century, but it was less than twenty years ago that the University of Texas started experimenting with growing grapes by drip irrigation on unused West Texas lands. Today there are 28 vineyards in Texas, most relative newcomers, although one, Val Verde Winery of Del Rio, is the hundred-year-old granddaddy of the business. The largest Texas winery, Ste. Genevieve, outside Fort Stockton, is in fact owned by a *French* corporation—the ultimate compliment to Texas' rejuvenated wine industry.

Woodpecker, ivory-billed

The largest North American woodpecker, it was frequently observed by John James Audubon in 1837 near Houston's Buffalo Bayou. The males he sighted were about eighteen inches long, with a prominent red crest as well as the advertised white bill (it is not made of ivory, of course, but was only the color of ivory). But the bird Audubon noted in such abundance was last photographed a hundred years after he saw it, and additional reliable sightings have been rare. Ornithologists agree, by and large, that the ivory-billed woodpecker is extinct. Yet it is still listed in bird guides, and among birders rumors persist that the elusive woodpecker is still hiding out in Texas.

XIT Ranch

Texas' second most famous spread after the King Ranch, the historical XIT no longer exists today. It was created in 1885 by a syndicate called the Capitol Freehold Land and Investment Company, a group of Illinois investors who, in return for building a new state capitol, received 3,050,000 acres in the western Panhandle from the State of Texas. At the time it was considered the largest ranch in the world, but in fact, another Panhandle ranch—the JA, owned by Charles Goodnight and Englishman John Adair—utilized (by leasing and other means) even more acreage—possibly as much as 20 million acres—though the ranchers did not actually own more than a million acres

In 1900 the XIT ran 150,000 head of cattle and had 335 windmills, 94 different pastures, and 7 separate headquarters. Cowboys strung up 1,500 miles of barbed wire fence, which as a single strand would have stretched 6,000 miles. A year later, though, the owners began to sell off land, and by 1929 the last of the XIT cattle was gone.

The best-known myth about the XIT concerns its brand, also the XIT. Cowboy folklore had it that the unusual trio of letters stood for "Ten in Texas," ten being either the number of counties that the ranch at least partially covered (which is true) or the number of investors in the syndicate (false). However, according to J. Evetts Haley's classic work, *The XIT Ranch of Texas*, the brand that gave the ranch its name was devised by veteran cowman Abner Blocker because the design was large and difficult to alter and required no specially made branding iron but merely five simple strokes of a single-iron. However, in Texas' most famous rustling story, clever criminals managed to blot, or alter, the XIT brand anyway. They ingeniously changed the XIT into the Star Cross, a six-pointed star with a slightly off-center cross inside it, where the letters *XIT* were disguised.

Y'all

The ubiquitous Texasism is a contraction of "you all," and as such is correctly spelled with the apostrophe after only the y. However, "y'all," like "barbecue," is frequently misspelled on signs or in books. The apostrophe is often misplaced as well, or downright ignored.

Although it is strictly speaking, plural, "y'all" is just as likely to be used in the singular.

Yankee

To a Texan a Yankee is not necessarily a resident of New England or New York City only. Anyone who lives north and east of Texas is a Yankee, though certainly residents of the Northeast are more apt to earn or deserve the label. Of course, the word "Yankee" also means an American, but you'll never hear a Texan, no matter how redblooded a patriot he is, using that particular synonym to describe himself.

Yellow jacket

This nasty wasp is actually more black than yellow, despite its name. The males rarely sting; the danger comes from the female of the species.

Yellow Rose of Texas

It was not a flower but a woman, and the lyrics of the classic Texas song don't begin to tell her story. Her name was Emily Morgan, and she was a mulatto belonging to a Texas landowner when, in April 1836, Santa Anna's troops rolled across Texas. Somehow the Mexican general laid eyes on the pretty slave girl, and he quickly claimed her as one of the spoils of war. According to the legend, he was so taken with the wench that he immediately ordered camp to be pitched at a less-than-ideal location between a bayou and the furious Texas Army, just so he could indulge himself in Emily's charms. You know the rest of the story: while Santa Anna slept, the Texans advanced and crushed his soldiers at San Jacinto. Thus did Emily Morgan become, as the song puts it, "the sweetest little rosebud that Texas ever knew." Texans like to think she knew full well that she was helping her new country by distracting the enemy from his proper goal—and that, no doubt, was why her eyes shone like the diamonds and sparkled like the dew. Thanks, Em.

Yucca

It is not a cactus but a member of the lily family. See **Cactus.**

Zapata County

Though the name of the South Texas county may call to mind the handsome and fiery Mexican revolutionary Emiliano Zapata, the county was actually named for a local pioneer and rancher called Antonio Zapata. The latter Zapata, a wealthy landowner, was exactly the kind of person that the revolutionary Zapata despised. Emiliano, by the way, though born in Mexico, was of Indian and not Mexican descent.

Zavala, Adina de

See **Driscoll, Clara.**

BIBLIOGRAPHY

Besides the indispensable *Texas Almanac*, published annually by the *Dallas Morning News*, and the Texas State Historical Association's exhaustive *Handbook of Texas*, references for *The Truth About Texas* include the following:

Adams, Ramon F. *Western Words*. Reprint. Norman: University of Oklahoma Press, 1981.

Barker, Eugene C. *The Life of Stephen F. Austin, Founder of Texas, 1793–1836*. Dallas: Cokesbury Press, 1925.

———. Charles Shirley Potts, and Charles W. Ramsdell. *A School History of Texas*. Chicago: Row, Peterson, and Company, 1921.

Bomar, George W. *Texas Weather*. Austin: University of Texas Press, 1983.

Burka, Paul, editor. *Texas, Our Texas*. Austin: Texas Monthly Press, 1986.

Cartwright, Gary. *Blood Will Tell: The Murder Trials of T. Cullen Davis*. New York: Harcourt Brace Jovanovich, 1979.

Dary, David A. *The Buffalo Book*. Chicago: The Swallow Press, 1974.

———. *Cowboy Culture*. New York: Alfred A. Knopf, 1981.

Dobie, J. Frank. *Apache Gold and Yaqui Silver*. Reprint. Albuquerque: University of New Mexico Press, 1976.

———. *The Longhorns*. Reprint. Austin: University of Texas Press, 1980.

———. *Rattlesnakes*. Boston: Little, Brown, and Company, 1965.

Elman, Robert. *Badmen of the West*. Secaucus, New Jersey: The Ridge Press/Pound Books, 1974.

Fehrenbach, T. R. *Lone Star*. New York: Macmillan, 1968.

Flexner, Stuart Berg. *Listening to America*. New York: Simon and Schuster, 1982.

Gard, Wayne. *The Great Buffalo Hunt*. Lincoln: University of Nebraska Press, 1968.

Graham, Don. *Cowboys and Cadillacs: How Hollywood Looks at Texas*. Austin: Texas Monthly Press, 1983.

Haley, J. Evetts. *The XIT Ranch of Texas and the Early Days of the Llano Estacado*. Norman: University of Oklahoma Press, 1953.

Hilton, Conrad. *Be My Guest*. Englewood Cliffs, New Jersey: Prentice-Hall, 1958.

Holmes, Jon. *Texas: A Self-Portrait*. New York: Harry N. Abrams, 1983.

———. *Texas Sport*. Austin: Texas Monthly Press, 1984.

Irwin, Howard S., and Mary Motz Wills. *Roadside Flowers of Texas*. Reprint. Austin: University of Texas Press, 1983.

James, Marquis. *The Raven*. New York: Bobbs-Merrill Company, Indianapolis, 1929.

Kennedy, Diana. *The Cuisines of Mexico*. New York: Harper and Row, 1972.

Lea, Tom. *The King Ranch*. Boston: Little, Brown, and Company, 1957.

Lifton, David S. *Best Evidence*. New York: Macmillan, 1980.

Loughmiller, Campbell and Lynn. *Texas Wildflowers*. Austin: University of Texas Press, 1984.

McCallum, Henry D. and Frances T. *The Wire That Fenced the West*. Norman: University of Oklahoma Press, 1965.

Newcomb, W. W., Jr. *The Indians of Texas*. Reprint. Austin: University of Texas Press, 1984.

Peña, José Enrique de la, *With Santa Anna in Texas*. Translated and edited by Carmen Perry. College Station: Texas A&M University Press, 1975.

Peterson, Roger Tory. *A Field Guide to the Birds of Texas and Adjacent States*. Boston: Houghton Mifflin, 1963.

Rosa, Joseph G., and Robin May. *Gun Law: A Study of Violence in the Wild West*. Chicago: Contemporary Books, 1977.

Schoelwer, Susan Prendergast. *Alamo Images: Changing Perceptions of a Texas Experience*. Dallas: DeGolyer Library and Southern Methodist University Press, 1985.

Smithwick, Noah. *The Evolution of a State, or Recollections of Old Texas Days*. Reprint. Austin: University of Texas Press, 1983.

Tarpley, Fred. *1001 Texas Place Names*. Austin: University of Texas Press, 1980.

Tennant, Alan. *The Snakes of Texas*. Austin: Texas Monthly Press, 1984.

Thompson, Thomas. *Blood and Money*. Garden City, New York: Doubleday, 1976.

Vines, Robert A. *Trees, Shrubs, and Woody Vines of the Southwest*. Austin: University of Texas Press, 1960.

Watts, Peter. *A Dictionary of the Old West, 1850–1900*. New York: Alfred A. Knopf, 1977.

Webb, Walter Prescott. *The Texas Rangers: A Century of Frontier Defense*. Reprint: Austin: University of Texas Press, 1985.

Wiley, Nancy. *The Great State Fair of Texas: An Illustrated History*. Dallas: Taylor Publishing Company, 1986.

Wolfenstine, Manfred R. *The Manual of Brands and Marks*. Norman: University of Oklahoma Press, 1970.

In addition, the author used numerous publications, most notably issues of the *Southwestern Historical Quarterly* and *Texas Monthly* magazine.

More Laughs from
 Gulf Publishing Company

How to Be Texan
Michael Hicks
Whether you're a Yankee, a Southerner, a Texan, or simply one of the great unwashed, this outrageous best-seller is the ideal guide to Texans.
66 pages, illustrations, paperback. ISBN 0-932012-21-3   #0221   **$8.95**

Cowboy Tales
Featuring the Debut of Hank the Cowdog!
John R. Erickson
These hilarious short stories reflect on the trials and tribulations of a Texas cowboy. This book introduces the star of Erickson's acclaimed series, Hank the Cowdog, in "Confessions of a Cowdog"!
96 pages, 5 1/2" x 8 1/2" paperback. ISBN 0-87719-257-X   #9257   **$6.95**

Cowboys Are Old Enough To Know Better
John R. Erickson
In this collection of short, thoughtful pieces, Erickson writes of cowboys, horses, cattle, dogs, kids, pranks, and roping a fiberglass horse in the Library of Congress!
104 pages, 5 1/2" x 8 1/2" paperback. ISBN 0-87719-256-1   #9256   **$6.95**

Cowboys Are Partly Human
John R. Erickson
I have an idea that a cowboy's best friend is a chiropractor. And that goes a long way toward explaining why cowboys walk funny. This and many other hilarious truths await you in twenty-two of Erickson's best short pieces on cowboy life.
100 pages, 5 1/2" x 8 1/2" paperback. ISBN 0-9608612-4-6   #6124   **$6.95**

Cowboys Are a Separate Species
John R. Erickson
Witty and often reflective, each Erickson piece is an entertaining look at the world through the unique perspective of a High Plains cowboy.
96 pages, 5 1/2" x 8 1/2" paperback. ISBN 0-916941-18-3   #4118   **$6.95**

Visit Your Favorite Bookstore!

Or see next page for an order form. ➡